TASTE OF THE TRIANGLE

TASTE OF THE TRIANGLE

A Guide to the Finer Restaurants of Raleigh, Durham, Cary and Chapel Hill with Recipes

JULI BROWN

WITH MAURA CLAVIN

DOWN HOME PRESS, ASHEBORO, N.C.

First Printing — April, 1997
1 2 3 4 5 6 7 8 9

ISBN 1-878086-56-1

Library of Congress Catalog Card Number
97-066333

Printed in the United States of America

Cover design by Tim Rickard
Cover and inside photography by Doug Pitts, except for city skyline photos which are courtesy of the *News & Observer*, Raleigh, N.C.
Book design by Beth Glover

Triangle chefs featured on the cover are: (back row l to r) Corey Mattson, Fearrington House; Richard Hege and Scott Cole, Margaux's; (front row l to r) Brack May, Pop's; Andrew Booger, Portobello; Jackie Berey, La Residence; Scott Howell, Nana's; Brian Stapleton, Il Palio Ristorante; and John Toler, Bloomsbury Bistro.

Down Home Press
P.O. Box 4126
Asheboro, N.C. 27204

Acknowledgements

This has been such a personal challenge and triumph that I feel I can not begin to thank every one involved. I will do my best.

Ashley Brown, Roger, Sabrina Nosal, and the staff at Margaux's, thank you for your unconditional enthusiasm and support. Also Maura Clavin, whose assistance was crucial, and Mark Houghtlin for his computer expertise.

Brian Cronin and Kristine Atkinson for the insightful wine notes.

Doug Pitts for sharing his photographic talents while allowing me style involvement.

Consultation thanks to Scott Cole and the entire Margaux's Staff, as well as John Toler of the Bloomsbury Bistro.

Jill Rutherford, Tracey Rawls, and Betty Shugart. Gwen Higgins and Hank Straus. Doug Russ, Alison J. Wilson, and Karl Ritz. John Toler. Bill Smith and Gene Hamer. Ronnie Swiller and Keith Foglemen. Corey Mattson, Heather Mendenhall, Eric Lampe and Susan George. Trey Cleveland. Devon Mills. Jackie Derey, Ben and Karen Barker and Liz Videau. Steven Horowitz and Richard Hege. Michael Schiffer, Gayle A White, Dane Johnston, Scott Howell, Brack May, Brian Stapleton, Andrew and Tara Booger, Alain Wellerstein, Paul Fontaine, Chris Bender, Suzan Goetchous, Even Lightner, Thor Johnson, Claud Rosini, and Scott Pigeon. Jay White. Bud and Mrs. Saylor. Norman and Mrs. Andrews. John Dorminey, and Dan Thomas. Blain Nierman. Richard, Rodolfo and Paolo De Martino. Mark Edelbaum and Brad Hurley.

FOREWORD

As a native Chapel Hillian of 40-plus years and a chef in the Triangle for the last 15, I've seen dramatic change and growth in our dining options.

The greatest impact has come in the way we consume; we have gone from dining out infrequently—typically after church on Sundays, on birthdays, holidays and special occasions—to eating restaurant food more often than we cook. Thus restaurants have become integral components of our lives, changing our tastes and making possible the many fine restaurants that we have now.

Two individuals made the greatest impact on this transition in the Triangle.

The first was Thad Eure, Jr., founder of the Angus Barn in Raleigh. Eure, the consummate restaurateur, recognized this shift in our habits in the '60s and realized that an establishment that offered quality meats, simply but expertly prepared, comfortable and gracious service, and a setting that was dramatic and different could serve a broad spectrum of clientele. His understanding of the needs of the business diner, without compromising the expectations of the special occasion diner, created an entity that continues to define the genre and is an ongoing success.

The second person was Bill Neal, who founded Restaurant La Residence in Chatham County in 1976. The enigmatic Neal defined the chef-proprietor as creator, director and technician while breaking new ground with changing, seasonal menus, sophisticated cuisine and elegant dining rooms. Neal not only recognized the community's need for sophisticated restaurant options, he also inspired a generation of chefs to create their own cuisines.

This book represents some of the finest examples of our burgeoning restaurant community and stands as evidence of the dramatic growth we have experienced in recent years. This trend will only continue and a compilation a year from now, or a year after that, would have new representatives of our vibrant and dynamic region. The Triangle diner is the beneficiary.

Ben Barker — Magnolia Grill, Durham

INTRODUCTION

Thank you for your interest in this book. I hope you will enjoy it as much as I have enjoyed putting it together.

I am pleased to say that it is the first of it's kind in the Triangle, a guide to Triangle dining as well as a recipe collection.

The population of the Triangle has reached an all-time high of more than 1/2 million and is estimated to grow to 1.2 million by the year 2005. Along with our growth has come the birth of many wonderful eateries, some of which are gaining national recognition.

These restaurants are a new breed, offering original, quality dishes for the same price you might pay at a chain where foods may be pre-processed or previously frozen. The chefs running these establishments are well educated and intent on breaking boundaries.

As Corey Mattson of the Fearrington House puts it, "This is the first time in history chefs are not required by the public to simply reproduce the classics; we are creating our own cuisine."

I was lucky to get one of the country's most creative chefs, Ben Barker of the Magnolia Grill, to provide the foreword to this book. He has been called the greatest chef in North Carolina but insists there are many in this area of his caliber. His own success has helped to create possibilities for others. Many fine restaurants have been opened by people who previously worked for Ben and his wife, Karen.

I have been honored to work with many of these talented people and am still in awe of their abilities and their dedication to their customers.

The chefs who participated in this project were given the freedom to share recipes of their choice. They spent much time preparing them so that even beginning cooks can create them at home. The wine selections were made by Brian Cronin, a talented sommelier who spent many years in our area and is now at Chicago's renowned Charlie Trotters, and Kristine Atkinson of Mutual Distributing Co. Most of these wines can be found in shops such as The Wine Merchant, A Southern Season, or Grapes, Beans and Hops—just to name a few.

I should note that many recipes in this book include stocks as an ingredient. There is no getting around their use in truly great cooking. Recipes for stocks as well as some standard sauces can be found in the recipe index. Some acceptable prepared stocks are now on the market and can be found at specialty stores such as A Southern Season and Wellspring.

It also should be noted that oriental ingredients are becoming increasingly popular and are often featured in this book. A visit to an oriental food store can help familiarize you with some of these. In some recipes the chefs offer alternatives for stocks or hard-to-find ingredients.

Recipes requiring advance preparation are marked as such. It is best to read through a recipe entirely before attempting it.

Enjoy!

Contents

ABBREVIATIONS KEY

Abbreviations used in restaurant information sections of this book

Entertainment: E
Vegetarian selections available: V
Private dining available: P
Outdoor dining available: O
Late night menu available: L
Smoking options:
    Smoking section available: A
    Non-smoking only: N
Reservations:
    Suggested: S
    Large parties only: LP
Attire:
    Casual: C
    Nice/casual: NC
    Dress suggested: D
Average dinner prices:
    1-$5-10
    2-$7-13
    3-$10-15
    4-$13-17
    5-$15-20
    6-$17-25
    7-$25+
Credit cards:
    American Express: Amex
    Diner's Club: Din
    Discover: Dis
    Master Card: MC
    Visa

Raleigh

Restaurants

ANGUS BARN

Address: 9401 Glenwood Ave., Highway 70 at Aviation Parkway
Phone: 787-3505
Hours: Monday-Saturday 5-11 p.m. Sunday 5-10 p.m.
     Lounge opens daily at 4 p.m.
E,V,P,A,S,NC,6
Credit cards: Amex/Din/Dis/MC/Visa

The Angus Barn is a Raleigh landmark, and its high standards have remained the same as when Thad Eure Jr. first opened its doors in 1960.

The original barn held only 200 diners, but after a fire destroyed the building in 1964, Eure built a bigger, better facility that now employs 200 and can serve up to 600.

This restaurant is almost a small village. The Wild Turkey Lounge holds up to 125 people and has entertainment most Fridays and Saturdays. There is the exclusive wine cellar dining room that holds 28; its only entrance is through the kitchen and down a set of winding stairs. The room has a 30-foot hand-carved table, 100-year-old tapestries and a large fireplace. Next to it is the temperature- and humidity-controlled wine cellar itself, which holds 1,000 different wines, including the notorious Jordan collection with a hefty price tag of $47,000. The wine list itself has gained national attention.

The Angus Barn serves more than 600 pounds of beef daily, and is adding its own meat processing plant to maintain freshness and quality. Beef, however, is not the only item on the menu. Seafood, lamb, pork and combination platters are also available.

Spinach Salad with
Warm Poppy Seed Dressing

Serves 4

Salad:

	fresh spinach (about 1 lb.)
1	small red onion, thinly sliced
2	boiled eggs, sliced
1 cup	fresh mushrooms, thinly sliced
8	slices cooked bacon, crumbled
	croutons

Poppy seed dressing:

1 cup	honey
1 1/4 tsp.	salt
1/2 cup	vinegar
1 1/4 cup	vegetable oil
1 TB	minced onion
2 tsp.	poppy seeds

• **PROCEDURE**

Thoroughly clean and dry spinach. Toss all salad ingredients.

Dressing:

Whisk all ingredients together. Slowly warm dressing and mix thoroughly before drizzling over salad.

Chef: Betty Shugart

Angus Barn Cheesecake

Yields 1 cheesecake

Crust:

1/4 cup	sugar
1/4 cup	melted butter
1 1/2 cup	graham cracker crumbs

Cheese Cake:

5	8-oz. packages cream cheese at room temperature
1/4 tsp.	vanilla
1 3/4 cup	sugar
3 TB	flour
1/4 tsp.	salt
4 or 5	eggs (about 1 cup)
2	extra egg yolks
1/4 cup	whipping cream

• **PROCEDURE**

Crust:

Mix all ingredients and press to the bottom and half way up the sides of the pan. Bake at 350 degrees for about 8 minutes and cool.

Cheesecake:

Preheat Oven to 300 degrees.

— Beat the cream cheese, sugar, salt, and flour until creamy. (It is very important never to over beat a cheesecake. Mix only until well blended. (Too much air in the batter will cause the cake to fall and crack after it has cooked.) Add the vanilla and the eggs and yolks one egg at a time, again not over beating.

— Pour into the baked crust. If you are using a spring form pan, wrap the bottom with foil. Place in a larger pan and add about 3/4" water surrounding the cheese cake. Place on a low rack in the oven and bake for 1 hour and 40 minutes.

• For a cappuccino cheesecake, simply add 1/2 oz. of cappuccino compound to the above recipe.

Chef: Betty Shugart

Sawdust Pie

Yields 1 pie

1	unbaked pie crust
1 1/2 cup	graham cracker crumbs
1 1/2 cup	flake coconut
1 1/2 cup	pecans, chopped
1 1/2 cup	sugar
7	egg whites, unbeaten

• **PROCEDURE**

Preheat over to 350 degrees.
— Combine all ingredients except pie crust until well mixed. Pour into unbaked pie shell and bake 35 minutes. Cool. Top with banana slices and whipped cream.

Chef: Betty Shugart

The Angus Barn

BLACK MARLIN

Address: 428 Daniels St., Cameron Village
Phone: 832-7950
Hours: Lunch: Monday-Saturday 11-4 p.m.
Dinner: Monday-Thursday 4 p.m.-10 p.m.
Friday-Saturday 4 p.m.-11 p.m.
E,V,P,A,S,NC,6
Credit cards: Amex/Din/Dis/MC/Visa

The Black Marlin, a sister restaurant to Cappers, is a Raleigh mainstay. The Black Marlin is an elegant, romantic spot with entertainment three times a week (call ahead for times).

The menu changes bi-monthly but may carry some items featured regularly. Don't let the name fool you. Lots more than seafood can be found here. You may find unique starters such as Oysters a la Marlin, which are brandy-flamed select Louisiana oysters topped with Reggiano cheese, shallots and spinach, or a standard favorite such as Baked Crab and Artichoke Dip. Entrees include everything from Pan-seared Rainbow Trout to lamb, Cornish hen, and even venison. Specials change daily and almost always include something exotic, such as ostrich or wild boar.

Black Marlin recently acquired a talented new chef, Alison J. Wilson, after the previous chef, Doug Russ, moved to the Midwest. Karl Ritz, the co-owner of Black Marlin chose to share a few of Doug's more interesting recipes, as well as Alison's.

Alison, originally from New York, is a graduate of the Culinary Institute of America. Her mother worked for General Foods and published her own cook books. When her parents chose to retire in the Triangle, she decided to follow. She began her work at the Fearrington House. She loves creating soups and sauces, and takes special satisfaction in combining generally unrelated ingredients to create something new and wonderful.

— recipes shared —
CREAM OF MUSHROOM & SHERRIED CRAB SOUP
TUNA CARPACCIO WITH SOY DIPPING SAUCE
PLANTAIN CRUSTED ALASKAN HALIBUT WITH TARRAGON BUTTER
CAJUN STUFFED FILET MIGNON
LIGHTLY DUSTED LEMON PEPPERED SALMON WITH CHAMPAGNE DILL BEURRE
BLANC FINISHED WITH SMOKED SALMON AND CAVIAR

Cream of Mushroom and Sherried Crab Soup

Yields about 1 gallon

3 lb.	mushrooms with stems
1/4 cup	shallots, minced
3 cups	sherry
	vegetable stock (enough to cover the mushrooms)
1 cup	fresh parsley, chopped
2 lb.	crab claw meat, picked and cleaned
1-2 qt.	heavy cream
	salt and pepper to taste
	roux if necessary

• PROCEDURE

Place mushrooms in food processor and pulse until roughly chopped. Put mushrooms, shallots and sherry in a large pot, pour the stock until it just covers mushrooms, and bring to a boil until it reduces a bit. Add the cream. (More or less can be added to your taste.) Add crab meat and season with salt and pepper. If it is too thin, thicken slightly with roux and mix in fresh parsley. Let heat completely and serve.

Chef: Alison J. Wilson

19

Tuna Carpaccio with Soy Dipping Sauce

Serves 4

2 lb.	sushi grade tuna
1 cup	freshly ground black peppercorns
1/4 cup	black sesame seeds (found in oriental markets)
	salt to taste

Dipping sauce:

1 1/2 cups	soy sauce
2 tsp.	finely diced carrots
1/2 tsp.	bonita flakes (found in oriental markets)
	juice of 1 lime
	sesame oil to taste
2 TB	freshly snipped chives
2 tsp.	golden sesame seeds
	juice of 1 lemon

• **PROCEDURE**

Cut tuna into 2-3-inch diameter logs. Mix cracked peppercorns, sesame seeds and salt together. Rub tuna logs evenly with sesame oil and dredge in peppercorn mixture. Sear the tuna evenly on all sides in well-oiled hot pan (the pan must be extremely hot before you pour in oil and sear tuna).

— Remove the tuna and chill to stop the cooking and firm the fish.

• **WINE SELECTION**

This dish calls for a delicate wine to complement the tuna lightly, as you do not want to cover up the intrinsic quality of the fish. A dry German Riesling, particularly, the Piesporter Goldtropchen from Von Kesselstat would be perfect. It has a light peach fruit beginning and a pronounced mineral finish, yet will not be overpowering for the tuna.

Chef: Doug Russ

Cajun Stuffed Filet Mignon

Serves 4

4	10-oz. filet mignon steaks

Stuffing:

1 cup	cooked baby shrimp
1/2 cup	andouille sausage, diced small
3 TB	whole grain mustard
1/4-1/2 cup	fresh bread crumbs
1	shallot finely chopped

Cajun cream sauce:

1/4 cup	onion, diced small
1 tsp.	Cajun seasonings
1 tsp.	jerk seasonings
1/2 cup	white wine
2 cups	heavy cream

• PROCEDURE

Make a 1-inch slit in the side of the steak, cutting a large pocket throughout. Mix all of the stuffing ingredients. Stuff each filet with 1/4 of the stuffing. Season with salt and pepper.

Sauce:

Place all of the ingredients but the cream in a pot and reduce over medium heat. Add the cream and bring to a boil. Thicken slightly with roux if necessary and season with salt and pepper to taste.

• TO SERVE

Grill the filets to the desired temperature and drizzle with the cream sauce.

Chef: Alison J. Wilson

Lightly Dusted Lemon Peppered Salmon with Champagne Dill Beurre Blanc finished with Smoked Salmon and Caviar

Serves 4

4 tsp.	flying fish caviar, or your choice
4 slices	smoked salmon
4	8-oz. salmon fillets
	lemon pepper seasoning
	cooking oil

Sauce:

1 cup	champagne (any brut will do)
1 TB	shallots, minced
2-3 TB	fresh dill, chopped
1 lb.	butter cut into 1-inch cubes
	salt and pepper to taste

• PROCEDURE

Sauce:

Place shallots and champagne in a pot and reduce until about 1/4 cup of the liquid remains. Let cool for 3-5 minutes, then whisk in the butter in three stages until it is melted but not separated. Add dill, salt and pepper to taste.

• TO SERVE

Lightly coat the salmon with oil and sprinkle with lemon pepper seasoning. Pan sear to desired doneness. Top each fillet with about 1 TB of champagne butter. Roll a piece of the smoked salmon and place it on the salmon and top with a dollop of caviar.

• WINE SELECTION

This lovely entree with its fabulous dill, champagne beurre blanc would match incredibly well with a white Grave from the Bordeaux region of France. All of the complex flavors call for a rich wine. A good suggestion would be Chateau Carbonnieux 1993 Graves.

Chef: Alison J. Wilson

Plantain Crusted Alaskan Halibut with Tarragon Butter

You will find plantains in most produce departments. The more yellow or red, the sweeter they will be. Doug suggests serving this dish with sweet potatoes and braised green beans.

Serves 6

3/4 lb.	plantains, cut into 1/2-inch slices on the bias
3 lb.	halibut fillets, cut into 8-oz portions
	salt and pepper to taste
1 cup	white zinfandel wine

Tarragon butter:

1 TB	shallots, julliened
4 tsp.	tarragon, chopped
1/2 cup	white wine
8 TB	unsalted butter
	salt and pepper to taste
1 tsp.	chives, snipped

• PROCEDURE

Soak the plantain slices in the white zinfandel for 24 hours, tossing occasionally to ensure they have fully marinated. Arrange chips on the halibut so as to form a crust and broil at 450 degrees until lightly golden and crisp. Bake at 325 degrees until cooked throughout. (No more than 15 minutes.) Serve with tarragon butter.

Butter:

Saute shallots with 1 TB butter. Deglaze pan with white wine. Add chives and tarragon. Add butter slowly, then add the salt and pepper to taste.

• WINE SELECTION

The dish is wonderful with a great Sonoma chardonnay. For example, Gallo Estate Chardonnay 1993, which is probably one of the best chardonnays. It is quite fruity and has a wonderful toasty oak finish, even a pronounced earthiness that is hard to find with most American wines. It pairs very well with the tarragon and the plantains.

Chef: Doug Russ

BLOOMSBURY BISTRO

Address: 509-101 Whitaker Mill Rd. at Five Points
Phone: 919 834-9011
Hours: Monday-Saturday 5:30-10 p.m.
V,A,S,NC,4
Credit cards: Amex/MC/Visa

A mural of the old Bloomsbury Park on the back wall sets the tone of Bloomsbury Bistro. Lace curtains, linen-clad tables and fresh flowers on each table enhance the feeling of elegance, which is complemented with the view of the steeple of Hayes Barton Church from the front window.

With 60 seats, the Bistro fairly bursts at the seams almost nightly.

Owner and Chef John Toler was born into a West Virginia coal mining family that also owned a trout hatchery, and John got a degree in fresh water fisheries before deciding that his real love was cooking. He entered L'Acadimie de Cuisine in Washington, D.C., and apprenticed at Cafe Bethesda and Occidental in Washington. He worked for two years at Mondo Bistro in Chapel Hill before moving to Raleigh and opening Bloomsbury Bistro in the spring of 1995.

John has an intuitive sense of flavor and the dishes from his kitchen show it. Starters may include Ragout of Wild Mushroom and Tomatoes with fresh Grilled Brioche and Aged Parmesan, Roasted Quail with Mustard Persilliade and Field Pea Salad, or the very popular Wilted Spinach Salad with Applewood Smoked Bacon, Smoked Gouda and Warm Honey-cider Vinaigrette. Entrees you may find are Spicy Leg of Lamb with Hummus Potato Puree and Roasted Eggplant Sauce, Crispy Leg of Duck Confit with White Beans, Kalamata Olives and Fennel Sausage, or Sauteed Carolina Red Snapper with Maine Lobster, Herbed

Pecan Rice and Tarragon Veloute.

Bloomsbury's wine list offers 12-15 selections by the glass or half glass.

— recipes shared —
CREAM OF FIVE ONION SOUP WITH CHIVES
ROASTED GAME HENS WITH BLACK OLIVE SPIKED MASHED POTATOES
AND WARM GOAT CHEESE VINAIGRETTE
PAN SEARED TUNA WITH CURRIED CITRUS VINAIGRETTE
AND SPICY COUS-COUS SALAD
ESPRESSO FLAN WITH KAHLUA AND CREAM

Cream of Five Onion Soup with Chives

Serves 6

4 TB	butter
2	shallots, finely chopped
4	cloves garlic, minced
2	large white onions, chopped
4	large Spanish yellow onions, chopped
1 qt.	chicken stock
1	large russet potato, peeled and chopped
1/4 cup	dry sherry
1 pt.	heavy cream
1 TB	fresh thyme, chopped
	salt and pepper to taste
2 TB	fresh chives, chopped

• **PROCEDURE**

Melt butter on medium heat in a heavy-bottomed, 6-qt. pot. Add shallots, garlic, and both onions and stir to coat with butter. Maintain heat and slowly cook the onions while stirring until they release their juices. Turn heat to medium high and continue stirring every 2 minutes until the onions caramelize and become deep brown in color. Add the sherry while lightly scraping the sides. Add the chicken stock and the potatoes, then bring to a boil. Simmer for about 10 minutes or until the potatoes are tender. Add the cream and thyme and bring to a boil once again. Remove from heat. Puree the soup in a blender until smooth and season with salt and pepper to taste. Top lightly with fresh chives.

Chef: John Toler

25

Roasted Game Hens with Black Olive Spiked Mashed Potatoes and Warm Goat Cheese Vinaigrette

This recipe was one of John's first menu items and very successful. As you can see, John shares tips as well as recipes.

Serves 4

4	fresh Cornish game hens

Herb paste:

1/4 cup	olive oil
4	cloves garlic, minced
1 TB	fresh thyme, chopped
1 TB	fresh rosemary, chopped
1 TB	fresh sage, chopped
1 TB	fresh Italian parsley, chopped
	juice and grated zest of 2 lemons
1 TB	fresh ground pepper
1 1/2 TB	salt

Mashed potatoes:

7-8	medium russet potatoes, peeled
1 cup	half and half
1 cup	black olives (oil cured Lebanese or Kalamata), roughly chopped
1	clove fresh garlic, minced
	juice of 1 lemon
1/2 stick	unsalted butter, softened
	salt and pepper to taste

Vinaigrette:

2	fresh shallots, peeled
1 TB	dijon mustard
1/4 cup	white wine vinegar
1	egg yolk
1/2 cup	peanut or canola oil
5 oz.	soft goat cheese (preferably Montrachet style)
	salt and pepper to taste
	hot water
6-8	large basil leaves

• PROCEDURE
Herb paste:
Combine all ingredients and stir well to make a homogenous mixture.

Vinaigrette:
Using a blender (not a food processor), blend shallots, mustard, wine vinegar, and egg yolk until a smooth paste is formed, scraping down the sides of the blender as necessary. With the machine running, slowly drizzle in half of the peanut oil, drop by drop at first, then in a slow steady stream. You should now have something that resembles mayonnaise.

— Stop the machine and add half of the goat cheese. Turn the machine on and let the cheese blend into the vinaigrette. If it is too thick to incorporate add 1-2 TB hot water to thin it. With the machine still running, drizzle in the remaining oil, adding hot water if necessary to thin. Add the remaining cheese and blend until smooth. Turn the machine off an add the basil leaves, blend again just until the leaves are finely pureed (if you blend it too much the vinaigrette will turn green). Add salt and pepper to taste.

— This can be make up to three days in advance and kept refrigerated.

Mashed potatoes:
Making really good mashed potatoes requires three things:

— 1. A nice starchy potato such as a russet.

— 2. The proper equipment to puree the cooked potato. A potato ricer works very well. An old fashioned hand-held vegetable masher works fine, but you will inevitably have lumps. The ideal machine is a stationary electric mixer with a wire whisk attachment. Do not use a food processor. It purees the potatoes too much and you will end up with something resembling wallpaper paste.

— 3. Getting as much half and half and butter as possible absorbed into the potatoes without them becoming runny. This is why you need a starchy potato like a russet.

— Place the whole, peeled potatoes in a pot just large enough to accommodate them and barely cover with cold water. Add 2 TB of salt and place the pot on high heat. Bring the water quickly to a boil, then turn the heat down and let the potatoes simmer until they are easily pierced with a knife. This will take about 25 minutes.

— While the potatoes are cooking, place the half and half, garlic and olives in a pot and bring the mixture to a simmer. Keep this mixture hot until the potatoes are cooked. This will allow time for the flavor of the olives to be released into the cream.

— When the potatoes are done, drain off all the water and allow them to air dry for 2-3 minutes. Place the potatoes in the bowl of the electric mixer and break them apart a little with a knife or fork.

27

— Begin whipping the potatoes with the whisk attachment, slowly at first so as not to whip them out of the bowl. Gradually increase the speed until the potatoes are whipped into a fluffy mass. Lower the speed to the slowest setting and gradually drizzle in the olive-flavored half and half. Once the potatoes have absorbed the half and half turn the machine off.

— Add the soft butter, lemon juice, and a pinch of salt and pepper. Turn the machine on low at first and gradually increase the speed to high. Whip the potatoes on high until they become fluffy and light, they will turn even more white in color as they are filled with air. Taste for salt and pepper and adjust seasoning. Keep the potatoes in a warm place until ready to serve.

• ROASTING THE HENS

It is extremely important to buy fresh birds. Those that have been frozen will lose most of their juices as they are roasted and become dry and tough.

— Preheat oven to 425 degrees.

— Remove any entrails and clip the wing tips from the hens. Rinse the hens in cool water and pat dry with a towel. Rub the herb paste evenly onto all the hens. Open the body cavity and coat the inside as well. Use kitchen twine to loosely tie the drumsticks to one another and do the same for the wings. Connect the wings by looping the string under the back and not across the breast.

— Place the hens on a wire rack set on a cookie sheet pan. This will allow the heat to flow under the hens as well and produce an evenly cooked bird. Place pan in oven.

— Game hens are small enough to cook in a hotter oven than you would need for a chicken. This will get skin nicely brown and crisp before the meat is overdone. Roast the hens for about 25 minutes and test for doneness. The breasts will be firm to the touch and the drumsticks should be loose in the socket. You can poke a small hole in the joint of the drumstick and the thigh and juices should leak out. When the hens are done, the juice should be clear. If any blood appears in the juice, return the birds to the oven for an additional five minutes. Use a knife or kitchen shears to remove the string from the hens.

— Heat vinaigrette slightly. A microwave will work great here. The vinaigrette will probably have thickened a little by now, so thin it to pourable consistency with a little hot water.

— Serve the hens perched upon the mashed potatoes. Spoon vinaigrette over and around.

Chef: John Toler

Pan Seared Tuna
with Curried Citrus
Vinaigrette and
Spicy Cous-cous
Salad

Pan Seared Tuna with Curried Citrus Vinaigrette and Spicy Cous-cous Salad

Serves 4

2	shallots, finely minced
	juice of 3 oranges
	juice of 2 lemons
	juice of 3 limes
1 TB	hot curry paste (available at most oriental markets)
1 TB	sambal oleick (available at most oriental markets)
3/4 cup + 2 TB	canola or peanut oil
3 TB	balsamic vinegar
1 tsp.	sugar
1 tsp.	fresh mint, chopped
1 tsp.	fresh basil, chopped
1 tsp.	fresh cilantro, chopped
	salt and pepper
4	fresh 7-8-oz. tuna steaks

Cous-cous salad:

2 cups	cous-cous
3 cups	water
1	red onion, finely diced
1/2 cup	golden raisins
1	ripe tomato, diced
1 TB	sesame seeds, toasted

• PROCEDURE

Vinaigrette:

In a large non-reactive bowl combine shallots with citrus juices, vinegar, sugar, curry paste, and sambal oleick. Lightly whisk together and allow the flavors to mingle for 15 minutes at room temperature. While constantly whisking, add the oil in a slow steady stream. This will create an emulsion and cause the vinaigrette to thicken. Stir in the chopped herbs and add salt and pepper to taste. Divide into equal halves and refrigerate.

Cous-cous salad:

In a 4-qt. (or larger) pot bring the water and 1 tsp. salt to a roiling boil. Remove the pot from the stove and pour in the cous-cous gradually; stir constantly. Cover the pot and place in a warm area for 10 minutes.

— After 10 minutes, place the cooked cous-cous in a large, non-reactive bowl. Use two forks to break the cous-cous apart into individual grains. Allow to cool at room temperature. Once cool, add the tomato, red onion, raisins and sesame seeds.

— Add one container of the reserved vinaigrette, tossing to coat the grains well. Refrigerate until ready to use. This can be made up to 24 hours in advance if kept refrigerated.

— Five minutes before serving, divide the cous-cous salad evenly onto four chilled plates and drizzle the remaining vinaigrette over and around the salad.

Tuna:

Place a heavy-bottomed saute pan over very high heat. While the pan is heating, remove any moisture from the tuna with paper towels. Generously salt and pepper both sides of the fish. Working quickly, add 2 TB of oil to the pan. Just as the oil begins to smoke, carefully add the fish steaks one at a time to the pan (for 1-inch thick steaks, cook approximately 1 minute per side for medium rare). Remove fish and towel off any remaining oil. Place fish over salad and serve immediately.

• WINE SELECTION

Trimbach Gewurztraminer from Alsace will go incredibly well with this dish. It's not too intense to mask the fish and has a great mineral quality for the cous-cous. The light spice produced by this fascinating grape enhances the tuna as well as the citrus. Alsace wines always work with tuna.

Chef: John Toler

Espresso Flan with Kahlua and Cream

This is a beautiful and elegant dessert.

Serves 6

3/4 cup	coffee beans, roughly ground, dark roasted
1/4 tsp.	nutmeg
1/4 tsp.	vanilla
	zest of 1/2 lemon, finely chopped
2 cups	heavy cream
1 cup	2% milk
1/2 cup	sugar
1/4 cup	brown sugar
3	egg yolks
2	eggs
1 cup	sugar
1/2 cup	water
1 cup	heavy whipping cream (very cold)
1 tsp	vanilla extract
2 TB	sugar
1 TB	Kahlua or coffee flavored liqueur

• **PROCEDURE**

Preheat oven to 295 degrees.

— Combine cream, milk, white and brown sugars, vanilla, coffee and lemon zest in a non-reactive pot. Bring to a simmer and remove from heat. Cover and allow the coffee mixture to steep for 1 hour.

— While the mixture is steeping, make a caramel with the sugar and water as follows: Place sugar, 1/2 cup water and 1/2 tsp. lemon juice in a heavy-bottomed 1- or 2-qt. pot. Place over medium heat and stir until sugar is dissolved. Allow to simmer undisturbed until the water is evaporated and the sugar begins to color. Cook the sugar until it reaches a deep amber color. Carefully pour 1 TB of the caramel into each of 6 5-oz. ovenproof ramekins. Place the ramekins in a shallow roasting pan and fill the pan with water to a level of 1-inch high on the ramekins.

— Place the eggs and the yolks in a small non-reactive bowl. Ladle 4-5 oz. of the warm coffee mixture into the eggs and gently whisk together. Pour the egg mixture back into the coffee mixture and briefly whisk to incorporate. Ladle this mixture through a fine mesh strainer. Fill each caramel-coated ramequin to within 1/8 inch of being full with the custard. Place the water-filled roasting pan and the custards into preheated oven.

— Bake for approximately 45 minutes or until the custards are set. They should be firm in the center and no longer jiggle when you tap the side of the ramequin. Remove them from the water bath, being careful not to get water in them. Place the custards in the refrigerator and allow them to cool completely. This can be done up to two days in advance.

— Add the sugar and vanilla extract to the heavy cream and whip to soft peaks. Finally, add the Kahlua and stir to incorporate.

— When you are ready to serve, remove the custards from the fridge. Use a thin-bladed knife to loosen the custard from the ramequin by running the blade around the entire inner surface of the glass. Place the ramequin upside down on a chilled serving plate.

— It is tricky to get the custard to free itself from the ramequin. Try this technique. Grasp the plate from the bottom with your fingertips and use your thumbs to hold the ramequin in place. Keeping everything level, jerk the plate in a quick motion and then jerk it abruptly back in an upward motion. This might take a few attempts but eventually you will hear and feel the custard release itself. Simply pull the ramequin off and allow the caramel to run freely around the plate. Spoon a big dollop of the Kahlua over the custard and serve.

Chef: John Toler

Espresso Flan with Kahlua and Cream

CAFE TIRAMISU

Address: 6196-120 Falls of the Neuse Rd.
Phone: 981-0305
Hours: Sunday-Thursday 5:30-10 p.m.
          Friday-Saturday 5:30-11 p.m.
V,A,S,NC,3
Credit cards: Amex/MC/Visa

Although it opened in November, 1996, Cafe Tiramisu's history extends back to Piccolo Mondo, a popular Raleigh restaurant for many years.

Paolo De Martino, owner and chef of Piccolo Mondo, was born and raised in Genoa, Italy, but he operated restaurants in Egypt, Cuba, Puerto Rico, New York and New Jersey before coming to the Triangle in 1976. Now his sons Richard and Rodolfo are following in his footsteps as the owners of Cafe Tiramisu, where Paolo now cooks (sometimes with both of his sons).

Although for sentimental reasons, the restaurant opened with an exact replica of the Piccolo Mondo menu, many new dishes have been added to the old favorites. You will find antipastis, insalatas and entrees such as authentic Lasagne, Fettuccine Carbonara, Osso Buco, Veal or Chicken Parmigiana. And to finish your experience, Paolo De Martino is said to have the best Tiramisu on the east coast.

The restaurant itself is small and quaint with contemporary atmosphere of dark colors, rod iron and elegant art.

— recipes shared —
Amatriciana
Pollo Alla Paolo
Eggplant Parmigiana

Amatriciana

Rodolpho recommends using linguini pasta for this dish as it will hold onto the ingredients with each bite, but any pasta will do.

Serves 4

4 cups	roma tomatoes, diced
1/2 cup	pancetta, diced
2 cups	white wine
4 TB	garlic, minced
4 TB	extra virgin olive oil
4 TB	basil
	fresh parmesan, grated
	salt and pepper to taste

• PROCEDURE

In a saute pan on medium-high heat, saute the pancetta with the olive oil and garlic until done. Add the tomatoes and saute for a minute more. Deglaze with the white wine. Let this simmer and reduce by half and add salt and pepper to taste. Toss the pasta with the fresh basil just before serving, then top with parmesan.

Chef: Paolo De Martino

Pollo Alla Paolo

Serves 4

4	large chicken breasts, cleaned and stripped of fat
1/2 cup	flour
2 TB	butter
	juice of 1/2 lemon
1/2 - 3/4 cup	heavy cream
8+	slices of prosciutto
8	slices of provolone
4	very large broccoli florets
	paprika

• **PROCEDURE**

Preheat oven to 375 degrees.

— Steam broccoli and set aside. Pound chicken breasts until thin and even. Dredge in the flour and lightly saute in butter on medium-high heat for 1-2 minutes on each side. When they are about done on the second side, sprinkle with lemon juice. Pour in cream and let simmer for a few minutes. You want this to be rather thick before serving. When this is done, construct the dinner by first placing in a baking dish the steamed broccoli, followed by the sliced prosciutto, then the provolone, followed by the chicken and cream. Bake for about 10 minutes and sprinkle with paprika before serving.

• **WINE SELECTION**

This wonderful chicken dish with its subtle lemon and cream sauce calls for a classic Bordeaux style white wine or a Meritage, which is a rich blend of grapes with complex flavors. A suggestion is the Guenoc Langtry, White Meritage 1995.

Chef: Paolo De Martino

Eggplant Parmigiana

Serves 4+

2	large egg plants
2	eggs, whisked
1/2 cup	flour
1 cup	Italian bread crumbs
1/2 cup	parmesan
about 12+	slices of fresh mozzarella
about 2 cups	fresh or bottled tomato sauce
4 TB	light oil

• PROCEDURE

Preheat oven to 350 degrees.

— Cut the eggplant into about 1/2-inch slices. You may remove the skins if you like. Dredge lightly in flour, then into the eggs, then into bread crumbs. Saute in the oil on medium-high heat until golden brown on each side. Gently dab the excess oil from the eggplant with a paper towel.

— To construct the dish, layer about 1/2-1 cup of tomato sauce in a 9x13-inch pan, then put 1 layer of eggplant. Sprinkle with most of the parmesan, reserving some for the final touch. Layer mozzarella next, then another single layer of eggplant. Top with tomato sauce. Bake for about 15 minutes or until it bubbles. Sprinkle with remaining parmesan.

Chef: Paolo De Martino

CAPPERS

Address: 4421 Sixforks Rd.
Phone: 787-8963
Hours: Lunch: Monday-Friday 11 a.m.-4 p.m.
**   Dinner: Monday-Thursday 5-10 p.m., late menu until 11**
**   Friday-Saturday 5-11 p.m., late menu until 12**
Jazz hours: Monday-Thursday 8-11 p.m.
**   Friday-Saturday 9 p.m.-1 a.m.**
E,V,L,A,S,NC,5
Credit cards: Amex/Din/Dis/MC/Visa

Few establishments greet their customers with so many smiles as do the employees of Cappers. Both the owner and chef take service seriously. "You can go quite a few places and receive a good meal but the service and atmosphere is what makes a place stand out," says Chef Ronnie Swiller, who often can be found wandering through the dining room checking on guests, who already are under the watchful eye of co-owner Keith Fogelman.

Born in Connecticut, Ronnie traces the beginning of his career back to age 13, when he and a friend began baking apple pies and selling them door-to-door. "Better than a lemonade stand," he says with a smile. "No one could resist."

At 18, he entered Johnson and Wales Culinary School in Rhode Island. His career since has taken him to Montana's Glacier National Park and a four-year stay in the Caribbean. His favorite dishes include seafood—"Only the freshest," he says—and this passion is reflected in Cappers menu.

Bouillabaisse and Baby Coho Salmon Stuffed with Crabmeat and Fresh Tomatoes, served over caramelized onions are just two of the items in his seafood spectrum. The menu is not limited to seafood, however. It includes a number of beef, lamb, poultry, pasta and veal selections. One of my favorites is Grilled Breast of Duck Served over Fresh Sautéed Spinach, Topped with a Roasted Garlic and Wild Mushroom Demi-glace.

The atmosphere at Cappers is city style with a cozy, casual feel, and don't forget the jazz, featured nightly.

— recipes shared —
Pesto Stuffed Portabella Mushroom en Croute
Grouper in Potato Horseradish Crust
Carpet Bagger
Thunderdome Pie

Cappers chef Ronnie Swiller with owners Keith Foglemen and Karl Ritz

Pesto Stuffed Portabella Mushroom En Croute

This is a very attractive appetizer. Serve whole or slice on the bias. You may use a demi-glace or a bordelaise over the dish or serve alone.

Serves 2-4

2	large portabella mushrooms

Marinade:

2 cups	balsamic vinegar
1 cup	olive oil
1/2 cup	parsley, chopped
1 TB	garlic, chopped
1 TB	shallots, chopped
	salt and pepper to taste

Pesto:

3 oz.	fresh basil leaves
1/2 cup	pine nuts, toasted
2 oz.	parmesan cheese, grated
4	garlic cloves
	juice of one lemon
1 1/2 cups	olive oil
	salt and pepper to taste

1	sheet puff pastry
	egg wash (2 whole eggs whipped with 2 TB water)

• **PROCEDURE**

Preheat oven to 350 degrees.

— In a stainless steel mixing bowl, blend all of the marinade ingredients and pour over the mushrooms. Let this sit for at least 1 hour.

Pesto:

In a blender or food processor add first five ingredients plus 2 TB of the olive oil and blend at high speed. Add olive oil slowly and in a steady stream. Consistency should be a little looser than mayonnaise. If you need to thicken, add more oil. Season with salt and pepper to taste.

Pastry:

Roll out puff pastry on a lightly floured cutting board so that it is large enough to cover mushrooms. Brush pastry with the egg wash and place first mushroom onto it cap side down. Dollop a large spoonful of pesto into the center of the mushroom and spread it around. Cut the pastry and bring it to the center to entirely cover the mushroom, sealing the seams with your fingertips. Flip over onto a greased baking sheet. Repeat the procedure with the second mushroom. Bake for 13 minutes.

Chef: Ronnie Swiller

Grouper in Potato Horseradish Crust

This unusual dish was inspired by Ronnie's grandmother. If you like heat, add extra horseradish or cayenne. The potato should be well squeezed or it will not adhere to the fish. If grouper is not available, snapper, sea bass or salmon may be substituted.

Serves 4

4	8-oz. boneless grouper fillets
4	large baking potatoes, unpeeled and cleaned
1/2 lb.	fresh chives, chopped
4 TB	horseradish
4	whole eggs
2 tsp.	cayenne pepper
	salt and pepper to taste

• **PROCEDURE**
Preheat oven to 350 degrees.
— In a small stainless steel bowl, grate potatoes using the largest holes on a hand-held grater. Place potatoes in a clean dish towel. Bring the ends together and squeeze over the sink until all the liquid has been removed. Mix all ingredients except grouper with potatoes. Test a small portion of potato mixture in a hot, lightly buttered skillet, and adjust seasoning.
— Pat the potato mixture as evenly as possible on the grouper fillets. You may have to squeeze it on. Cook each fillet for 4 minutes on each side in a medium-hot skillet with butter. Finish in oven for approximately

15 minutes.

• **WINE SELECTION**
This succulent grouper in combination with potatoes and horseradish calls for a medium-bodied chardonnay that contains a nice oak finish such as a Deloach OFS, Chardonnay 1994.

Chef: Ronnie Swiller

Carpet Bagger

Advance preparation required.
This is an impressive looking entree. Time is needed to prepare the bearnaise and demi-glace, both of which can be made from the recipe in the Stocks and Sauces section of this book. If this is not possible, I recommend calling a restaurant that serves bearnaise on a regular basis and ask to purchase a small portion. Do not use packaged bearnaise.

Serves 4

4	8-oz. center-cut filet mignon
8	16-to-20-count shrimp, peeled and deveined, tail cut off
8 oz	bearnaise sauce (see recipe in Index)
8 oz.	demi-glace (see recipe in Index)

Beer batter:
2 cups	flour
2-3	cans light beer
2	eggs
	salt
	white pepper
	garlic powder

• **PROCEDURE**
Grill filets to your liking. While filets are cooking, prepare beer batter.
— Place flour in a stainless steel bowl. Whip in beer and eggs in a slow steady stream. Whip until no flour balls are left. Add seasonings. This should be enough to coat shrimp well. Heat 4 cups vegetable oil to 325

degrees. When filets are just about ready, dip shrimp in batter and fry for about four minutes. When filets are finished, slice them in half horizontally. Place the first half on a bed of demi-glace, top with two fried shrimp and a dollop of bearnaise. Top with other half of filet.

• WINE SELECTION

This classic grilled filet and seafood dish with the delicate bearnaise sauce demands a mature, ready-to-drink, cabernet sauvignon such as a 1985 vintage. A great choice would be the Jordan, Cabernet Sauvignon, Sonoma 1985.

Chef: Ronnie Swiller

Carpet Bagger

Thunderdome Pie

This dessert, a regular at Cappers, features delicate and delicious cake layers with a rich mousse filling and Chantilly cream.

Serves 6-8

Cake:

3/4 cup	flour
1/2 cup	sugar
1/4 cup	sifted cocoa powder
1 tsp.	baking soda
1/2 tsp.	salt
1/2 cup	buttermilk
1/3 cup	oil
1/2 tsp.	vanilla
1	egg

Chocolate mousse:

1/2 lb.	chocolate coverture (or any other high quality, semi-sweet chocolate)
4 oz.	pate a bombe (recipe to follow)
2 cups	whipping cream

Pate a bombe:

1/2 lb.	granulated sugar
2 oz.	corn syrup
1/2 cup	water
5	large egg yolks
1 tsp.	salt
1 tsp.	vanilla

Chantilly cream:

2 cups	heavy cream
1-3 oz.	confectioners sugar

Chocolate cookie crumbs or shavings for garnish

• **PROCEDURE**

Cake:

Preheat oven to 325 degrees.

— Sift all the dry ingredients together and add the remaining ingredients. Blend on low speed until well moistened. Beat on medium speed for 3 minutes. Pour into two 9-inch, lightly greased pans dusted with cocoa. Bake for 35-45 minutes, using cake tester to check doneness.

Pate a bombe:
Heat sugar, corn syrup and water to 245 degrees (softball candy stage). In a separate large bowl, hand whisk the egg yolks, salt and vanilla. Pour the hot mixture in a slow stream into the egg yolks, whipping continually until the mixture has completely cooled.

Chocolate mousse:
Melt chocolate over a double boiler. Let cool at the same time pate a bombe is cooling. When cool, gently mix the two. Whip cream until somewhat stiff and gently fold into chocolate mixture. Chill in refrigerator for several hours.

• TO ASSEMBLE
Flip out cooled cakes. Pipe Chantilly cream around the edge of 1 layer to approximately 1 inch in height. Fill the center with chocolate mousse, forming a dome shape. Place second layer onto mousse, keeping dome shape. Cover entire cake with Chantilly cream. Sprinkle with chocolate cookie crumbs or fine chocolate shavings.

Chef: Iris Bockish

CLAUDIO'S

Address: 6300 Creedmoor Rd.
Phone: 847-0083
Hours: Monday-Friday 11:30 a.m.-10 p.m.
       Saturday 5-10 p.m.
       Lunch until 3 p.m.
V,A,S,C,3
Credit cards: Amex/MC/Visa

      Claud Rossini, owner and chef of Claudio's, looks and acts every bit Italian, and rightly so. He was raised in an Italian neighborhood in New Jersey by a traditional Italian family. Claud's grandfather insisted that only Italian be spoken in his home. As in any Italian family, food played a major role. Sunday dinners were planned by Wednesday and were attended by all family members.

      Claud's love of cooking goes back to age five, when he began helping his two grandmothers in the kitchen. One grandmother lived in his home and the other next door. What better teachers than two Italian grandmothers? Both had arthritis and Claud became indispensable to them.

      Family is still important to Claud. His wife Sandra and two daughters play a large part in the restaurant. You may find his oldest daughter greeting and seating guests.

      Claud has owned Claudio's for three years and is also part owner of Sorrento. Despite the responsibilities of ownership, Claud still will be found in the kitchen, preparing every dish "as if I were serving my own mother."

      Claud's menu selections include an appetizer of homemade mozzarella and roasted peppers baked in crust and topped with fresh tomato cream sauce, entrees such as Veal or Chicken Sorrentino Cutlets, sautéed and topped with prosciutto, eggplant, tomatoes and fresh mozzarella, in a delicate Marsala sauce. Vegetarians and seafood lovers will also find many choices. Claud has an extensive wine list that he continues to add to with the help of his staff.

— recipes shared —
Chicken a la Claudio
Rigatoni a la Vodka
Tiramisu

Chicken a la Claudio

Advance preparation required.
Despite that, this dish, is well worth the time. The reduction of stock and cheese for the sauce makes it rich and smooth. Bleu cheese may be substituted but gorgonzola is recommended.

Serves 4

4	boneless, skinless chicken breasts
2 TB	olive oil
2 tsp.	shallots, chopped
4 TB	gorgonzola cheese
2 TB	butter
2 cups	shitake mushrooms, sliced
1 1/3 cups	tomatoes, diced
1 1/3 cups	broccoli florets
1/2 cup	white wine
	salt, pepper, garlic powder to taste
3 cups	chicken stock (canned broth may be substituted)
3 cups	veal stock (canned beef broth may be substituted)

• PROCEDURE

Tenderize chicken breasts by pounding on shiny side until the same thickness throughout (this allows even cooking).
— Heat olive oil in a large saute pan on medium-high heat. Saute chicken on both sides until light brown. Remove chicken and set aside.
— Add butter to same pan and caramelize shallots. Add mushrooms.

When mushrooms are fairly soft, deglaze pan by adding white wine. Add veal and chicken stock. Season with salt, pepper and garlic powder to taste, then add cheese. Allow to reduce by half, add tomatoes, broccoli and chicken. When broccoli is done to your liking, preparation is complete. Serve immediately.

• **WINE SELECTION**

A Beaujolais style red dolcetto grape from Piedmonte, Italy would complement both the chicken and the gorgonzola. An excellent choice would be La Spinona, Delcetto 1994.

Chef: Claud Rossini

Rigatoni a la Vodka

This is one of Claud's most popular dishes. The combination of fresh tomato sauce and cream sauce makes for a rich and delectable dish.

Serves 4-6

6 TB	lightly salted butter
2 tsp.	shallots, chopped
1 1/2 cups	shitake mushrooms
1 1/2 cups	sun-dried tomatoes
3 cups	fresh tomato sauce (recipe follows)
2 oz.	vodka
3 cups	heavy cream
1 1/2 cups	half and half
1/2 tsp.	white pepper
1/2 tsp.	garlic powder
1/4 tsp.	salt
3 cups	early green peas (cooked and drained)
16 oz.	cooked rigatoni

Fresh tomato sauce:

12	large ripe tomatoes
1/2 cup	olive oil
3	cloves garlic, minced
1/4 tsp.	salt
1/4 tsp.	pepper

Tomato sauce:

Core and blanch tomatoes in boiling water until tender. Remove from water, drain and rinse in cold water. Remove the peel and crush well. Place crushed tomatoes in large sauce pan. In small saute pan, saute garlic in olive oil until garlic is light brown. Strain garlic from oil. Discard garlic and add oil to tomatoes. Cook tomatoes until reduced by half, about 1 hour. Season with salt and pepper.

Rigatoni:

In large saute pan saute shallots in butter until translucent over medium-high heat. Add mushrooms and sun-dried tomatoes and continue to saute until the mushrooms are soft. Deglaze pan with vodka and add fresh tomato sauce, heavy cream, and half and half. Add remaining seasonings and cook over medium heat, stirring occasionally until sauce thickens and reduces slightly. Add peas and when hot pour over rigatoni and serve immediately.

• WINE SELECTION

This traditional Italian dish with its fresh tomato and cream sauce will match well with an Italian red wine from Sicily. A top notch producer from that region is Regaliali, therefore a great accompaniment would be the Regaliali, Rosso 1994.

Chef: Claud Rossini

Tiramisu

Tiramisu is a traditional trifle-like Italian dessert known for it's delicate texture and strong espresso flavor. It is best to prepare this desert a day in advance. No cooking is necessary.

Serves 12

8	eggs separated
1 cup	sugar
1/2 oz.	sweet Marsala wine
1 oz.	vanilla extract
	cocoa powder
17 oz.	mascarpone cheese
24	lady fingers
2 cups	espresso
1 oz.	triple sec

• **PROCEDURE**

In a large mixing bowl beat together egg yolks, 1/2 cup sugar, Marsala and vanilla extract until frothy and pale yellow. Beat in the mascarpone cheese and refrigerate. In a separate mixing bowl, beat egg whites while slowly adding 1/2 the sugar until stiff peaks appear. Carefully fold the whites into the yolk mixture and refrigerate. Blend together triple sec and espresso. Dip each ladyfinger into the blend and lay them side by side on the bottom of a 9x13-inch glass dish. Cover the lady fingers with 1/2 of the custard. Add another layer of lady fingers and cover with remaining custard. Sprinkle the top with cocoa. Chill thoroughly before serving.

• **WINE SELECTION**

Banfi Moscato d'Asti is a sparkling, sweet, and refreshing wine that that accentuates the aromatic fruit and creamy cheese of tiramisu and adds an effervescence to this wonderful dessert.

Chef: Claud Rossini

DODD-HINSDALE
RESTAURANT AND TAVERN

Address: 310 Hillsborough St.
Phone: 829-3663
Hours: Restaurant: Monday-Saturday 5:30-10:30
Tavern open daily at 4:30
V,P,A,S,NC,4
Amex,MC,Visa

The Dodd-Hinsdale is an elaborately refurbished mansion in downtown Raleigh. Much attention was given to maintaining the decor and rich, intricate architectural details.

Downstairs, the tavern seats about 80 and serves six Micro-brew beers on tap in addition to an accommodating wine list. Patrons have a view of the attractive wine cellar. A separate bar menu includes a variety of light and heavy appetizers.

Upstairs, the dining room seats about 150. Private dining rooms are available as well. The menu features Southern and American fare, with dishes changing seasonally according to fresh ingredient availability.

Chef Daniel Schurr is a graduate of the Culinary Institute of America and worked five years at the Four Seasons Hotel in Philadelphia. He worked at Angus Barn before moving to Dodd-Hinsdale.

Although the Dodd-Hinsdale is extravagant, Daniel says the owners are trying for a casual atmosphere.

Rutabaga and Game Soup

This is a classic European-style soup. The bones remain in the soup throughout the process. A chinos is called for to strain the soup after its completion. This is a very fine mesh strainer. If you do not have this, try cheesecloth.

Serves 8

1/4 cup	olive oil
2 lb.	chicken or pheasant bones, rinsed and chopped
1 lb.	rutabagas, rinsed and chopped

Mirroix:

4 oz.	onions, peeled and sliced thin
2 oz.	whole garlic, rough chopped
1	celery stick, rough chopped
1	carrot, rough chopped
1/2 bunch	thyme, chopped

4 oz.	rice
3/4 gall	chicken stock
1/2 pt.	heavy cream
	salt and pepper to taste

• **PROCEDURE**

In a large braising pan, heat the oil until smoking. Add bones and season, brown well. Add mirroix and brown until tender, then add rutabagas and sweat until tender. Add chicken stock and rice, reduce heat and simmer for 1 1/2 hours. Add the heavy cream and simmer for another hour. Puree entire soup in a blender and strain through a chinos. Season with salt and pepper and garnish with fresh thyme.

Chef: Daniel Schurr

Roasted Swordfish Loin with Curried Potato Puree, Asparagus Tips and Parsley Sauce

Serves 2

10 oz.	swordfish
	salt and pepper to taste
	fresh lemon juiced
about 1lb.	fresh asparagus

Curry sauce:
2 TB	olive oil
1 oz.	onion
1 oz.	garlic
1	apple, chopped
2 TB	curry powder
3 cups	chicken stock
2 cups	heavy cream

Potatoes:
about 2	large Idaho Potatoes
	water
	salt, butter, and milk to taste

Parsley sauce:
1 TB	olive oil
1 oz.	onions
1 oz.	celery
1	garlic clove
2 bunches	parsley
1 qt.	chicken stock
	salt to taste
2 TB	heavy cream

• PROCEDURE
Fish:
Preheat oven to 400*
— Season the fish and heat the oil to smoking. Sear the fish on either side then finish in the oven for approximately 12 minutes. Splash the fish with lemon as you remove it from the oven.

Curry sauce:
Heat the oil in a sauce pot over medium-high heat and sweat the on-

ions, garlic, and chopped apple until tender. Add the curry and saute for another 8-10 minutes, being careful not to burn. Add the stock and reduce to about 1 cup. Add the cream and reduce again until thickened. Strain through a fine mesh strainer and set aside.

Potatoes:
Peel the potatoes and cut in quarters. Boil until tender and pass through a ricer. Add the butter, salt and milk to taste, making sure they are not too moist. Add about 1/2 cup of curry cream and mix.

Parsley sauce:
Blanch the parsley leaves, setting aside the stems, and puree in a blender. Set aside. Heat the oil and saute the onions, celery, garlic and parsley stems until tender. Add the chicken stock and reduce to 1 cup. Add salt and pepper and strain through a fine strainer and reserve. Whisk the parsley puree into the stock and add the heavy cream to finish the sauce.

• To SERVE
Cut the white ends off the asparagus and blanch. Spread on plates in a fan design. Spoon the potatoes in a pile on the center of the plate and lean the fish on the potatoes. Drizzle the sauce over the plate and serve.

Chef: Daniel Schurr

Chocolate Cream Brulee

Brulee is a classic custard-style dessert and chocolate is a pleasant change to the ever-popular vanilla. Traditionally, fresh berries of any kind are served alongside a brulee. Also when caramelizing the sugar, try raw sugar rather than processed.

Serves 7

1 qt.	heavy cream
1	vanilla bean
13	egg yolks
1 cup	sugar
8 oz.	bittersweet chocolate
1 cup	sugar for caramelizing
7	brulee molds

• PROCEDURE
Preheat oven to 325*
— Bring 1/2 cup sugar, cream, and vanilla bean to a boil. In a separate pan, melt the chocolate on very low heat. In a separate boil, whisk together the yolks and 1/2 cup sugar. Mix the chocolate with the cream mixture. Slowly add to this the yolk mixture. When well blended, pour into the molds. Cook in a water bath, (a pan with about 1/2 inch water on the bottom) for about 45 minutes or until firm. This process prevents the brulee from cracking. To serve, spread about 1 TB of sugar on the cooled brulee and broil until sugar caramelizes, being careful not to burn.

Chef: Daniel Schurr

518 WEST

Address: 518 West Glenwood Ave.
Phone: 829-2518
Hours: Lunch: Monday-Saturday 11:30 a.m.-2:30 p.m.
Dinner: Sunday-Wednesday 5-10 p.m.
Thursday-Saturday 5-10:30 p.m.
V,N,NC,3
Credit cards: Amex/Din/Dis/MC/Visa

518 West, which opened early in 1997, is the sister restaurant to 411 West in Chapel Hill. Like 411, 518 has spectacular decor: bright, open and airy with two levels of dining, seating more than 200.

Blain Nierman, head chef, worked for six years as executive chef of the South Carolina Country Club before moving to Raleigh to preside over 518's kitchen. A graduate of Johnson and Wales Culinary Institute in Rhode Island, Blain has a wide portfolio but his favorite dishes are seafood and vegetarian.

The menu is reasonably priced and contains items such as wood-fired pizzettes with uncommon toppings such as fontina cheese, beef tenderloin, marinated chicken and artichoke hearts. Salad choices include Wood Grilled Chicken, and Spinach Salad with Grilled Red Onions, Bacon and Tomatoes with a Honey Dijon Vinaigrette. Pastas are offered in full and half orders and include Lemon Linguini with Shrimp, Scallops, Tomatoes, Scallions, White Wine and Clam and Lobster Butter and Whole Wheat Fettucine with Chicken, Mushrooms, Rosemary Butter, Marsala, Cream and Fresh Parmesan. There are daily entree and dessert specials and the wine list is ample.

Apple Walnut Salad with Grilled Chicken and Gorgonzola with Cranberry Vinaigrette
Oven Roasted Fennel and Wild Mushroom Bruschetta with Toasted Pistachios and Pernod Cream Sauce
Sauteed Crab and Artichoke Cakes on Baby Greens with Chipolte Aioli

---

Apple Walnut Salad with Grilled Chicken and Gorgonzola with Cranberry Vinaigrette

Serves 4

Salad:

about 6 cups	mixed greens
4 oz.	cranberry vinaigrette
4	grilled chicken breasts
1	large apple, thinly sliced
1/4 cup	walnuts, toasted
1/2 cup	gorgonzola crumbles

Vinaigrette:

1/2 cup	cranberries
1/2 cup	balsamic vinegar
2 TB	sugar
2 TB	grilled red onion
2 tsp.	Dijon mustard
2 cups	olive oil

• PROCEDURE

Vinaigrette:
Combine cranberries, vinegar and sugar in a pan and heat to a boil. Pop the berries and cool. Place in blender and add the red onions and the Dijon. While this is blending, slowly drizzle in the oil until well emulsified.

Salad:
Toss the greens with the vinaigrette and place in individual salad bowls.

Grill the chicken and cool. Slice each chicken breast in 4-5 slices. Stagger the chicken and apple slices in a fan shape on the greens. Sprinkle the walnuts and gorgonzola evenly on each salad, drizzle with a bit more vinaigrette and serve.

Chef: Blain Nierman

Oven Roasted Fennel and Wild Mushroom Bruschetta with Toasted Pistachios and Pernod Cream Sauce

Blain suggests using a mix of shitake, portabella, or oyster mushrooms, but says any mix will do. For the bruschetta, a nice French or Italian loaf will work. Cut into thin, diagonal slices.

Serves 4

3 TB	oil
2 cups	wild mushrooms
2 cups	oven roasted fennel (procedure to follow)
	pinch salt and pepper
1 oz.	white wine
16 slices	grilled bruschetta
	Pernod cream sauce (recipe to follow)
1/2 cup	toasted pistachios
	parsley sprigs

Pernod Cream Sauce:

1 tsp	shallots, chopped
1/2 cup	white wine
1/2 cup	Pernod
1 cup	cream
4 TB	butter
pinch	pepper

Fennel:

4 cups	fennel, julienned
2 TB	oil
	salt and pepper to taste

• PROCEDURE

Fennel:

Toss the fennel in the oil and sprinkle with salt and pepper. Lay out on a sheet pan and roast in 375-degree oven for about 15 minutes.

— Purchase the pistachios toasted or place them in a 375-degree oven for 7-10 minutes or until lightly toasted.

— Lightly brush the bruschetta with olive oil and pan grill the bread until crisp.

— In a saute pan, heat the oil and lightly saute the mushrooms. Then add the roasted fennel and continue to saute for 1-2 minutes. Deglaze the pan with wine and sprinkle with salt and pepper.

Sauce:

In a pan on medium-high heat, reduce a mixture of the wine, Pernod, and shallots by half. Add cream and reduce again by half. Whisk in the butter and pepper.

• TO SERVE

Place the mushroom-fennel mixture on the grilled bruschetta and drizzle on the cream. Sprinkle with the pistachios.

• WINE SELECTION

It is difficult to match a wine to such strong flavors as Pernod and fennel so a Brut would be a better choice. A nice suggestion would be a Pol Roger Brut NV, Eperndy France.

Chef: Blain Nierman

Sauteed Crab and Artichoke Cakes on Baby Greens with Chipolte Aioli

Serves 4

Cakes:

1 lb.	back fin crab meat, picked and cleaned
2 cups	bread crumbs
1/2 cup	artichoke hearts, chopped
1 TB	fresh basil, chopped
2 TB	oregano, chopped
3 TB	sun-dried tomato, chopped
2 TB	olive oil
2	eggs, beaten
3 TB	water

Dish:

2 TB	oil
3 cups	baby greens
	Aioli (recipe to follow)
4	lemon wedges
	fresh parsley

Aioli:

1 cup	mayonnaise
2 tsp.	minced garlic
2 tsp.	lemon juice
1/2 cup	Chipolties in Adobo Sauce (This sauce can be found at Well Spring or Fresh Market, among other places)

• PROCEDURE

Cakes:

Lightly combine the crab meat, bread crumbs, artichoke hearts, basil, oregano, sun-dried tomatoes and olive oil. Add the beaten eggs and mix well. Adjust the moisture with water. In a large skillet, heat the oil on medium-high heat. Form cakes in an oval shape in the palm of your hands, no more than 1 1/2 inch in thickness. Press together lightly. Saute the cakes for 1-2 minutes on each side.

Aioli:

For the aioli, simply place all of the ingredients in a food processor and mix well.

• TO SERVE

Place the baby greens on the plates and two cakes on each plate. Drizzle the aioli over the cakes or serve it alongside as a dip. Garnish with lemon wedges and parsley.

Chef: Blain Nierman

42ND ST. OYSTER BAR

Address: 508 West Jones St.
Phone: 831-2811
Hours: Monday-Friday 11:30 a.m.-11 p.m.
        Sunday 5-10 p.m.
        Entertainment: Thursday-Saturday 10 a.m.-1 p.m.
E,L,A,C,3
Credit cards: Amex/Din/MC/Visa

The building currently known as the 42nd St. Oyster Bar has seldom sat empty since 1927. In 1931, J.C. Watson began serving oysters in what was then a grocery store. When prohibition ended in 1933, his was the first business in Raleigh to sell draft beer in frosted mugs, and the grocery gradually became a bar.

The place became known as the 42nd St. Oyster Bar after a group of doctors who were loyal customers spent time on New York's 42nd street while attending a convention. When they returned, the name was affectionately transferred and it stuck.

The business changed hands many times before closing in 1985. After that, the building sat vacant until the present restaurant opened in 1987 with help from noted Raleigh restaurateur Thad Eure. Co-owner Brad Hurley says the current success comes from the assortment of seafood offered.

It's not feasible to name everything on the menu, but suffice to say that oysters are served eight different ways, and that's just the beginning. Shrimp are served four different ways. Then there are clams, calamari, lobster, crab, halibut, catfish, scallops, and crab cakes. Not to mention soups, pastas, chicken, beef, and combination platters.

Steamed oysters and shrimp are served only at the shell bar, which is more than 50 seats long. The decor is nostalgic with its 1950 barstools, old-fashioned phone booths, memorabilia from the original bar, and open-air kitchen with a beautiful mural on the overhang.

Executive Chef Mark Edelbaum has been with the restaurant since its opening in 1987. He and his 150 co-workers maintain high standards.

— recipes shared —
Oriental Cucumber and Vidalia Onion Relish
Vogie's Cajun Ettouffee
Key Lime Pie

Kitchen staff of 42nd St. Oyster Bar

Oriental Cucumber & Vidalia Onion Relish

Good on chicken, grilled fish, or shrimp.

Yields about 1 pint

1 cup	Vidalia onions
1 1/2 cups	cucumber, diced
2 TB	red pepper, chopped
1 TB	sesame seeds, toasted
2 TB	fresh lime juice
1 TB	sesame oil, dark
1 TB	light soy
1 tsp.	sugar
1/8 tsp.	dry crushed red pepper
1/4 cup	green onion, chopped

• **PROCEDURE**

Cut and dice onions, cucumbers, and sweet red pepper. Mix and set aside.

— In a separate bowl mix lime juice, sesame seed oil, light soy sauce, sugar, and dry crushed red pepper. Add toasted sesame seeds. Mix onion/cucumber/red pepper mixture and green onions into dressing. Let marinade for at least 2 hours.

Chef: Mark Edelbaum

Vogie's Cajun Ettouffee

This dish is wonderful alone or with shrimp, chicken, or crawfish. Saute any one of the three and add the sauce. Finish with white wine butter, green onions and parsley over rice.

Serves 4

	Choice of meat to serve 4
1 cup	celery, finely diced
1 cup	onions, finely diced
1 cup	green peppers, finely diced
1 cup	clam juice
1 oz.	lobster base
2 tsp.	salt
1 tsp.	white pepper
1 tsp.	black pepper
2 tsp.	cayenne
1 tsp.	basil
pinch	thyme
1 tsp.	garlic powder
3/4 cup	salad oil
	flour (as needed roughly 1:1 w/oil)

• PROCEDURE

Heat oil in blackening pan until smoking. Add flour, remove from heat. Stir frequently until roux turns the desired dark brown color (10 minutes). Heat clam juice and lobster base in sauce pot. When roux is

Vogie's Cajun Ettouffee

desired color, add celery, onions, peppers, and 1 TB herb mixture. When veggies are done, add to boiling stock slowly while stirring. When sauce begins to thicken, add remaining spices. Simmer 25 to 30 minutes until flour taste disappears. Cool in ice bath.

Chef: Cliff Vogelsberg

Key Lime Pie

Yields 1 pie

5	egg yolks
1 can	condensed milk
1/2 cup	fresh lime juice
	graham cracker pie crust

• **PROCEDURE**

Preheat oven to 275 degrees.
— Whip egg yolks until stiff. Add condensed milk. Mix well. Pour in lime juice slowly as you continue mixing. Pour into pie shell and bake for 15 minutes. Remove from oven and cool.

Chef: Mark Edelbaum

Margaux's

Address: 8111-111 Creedmoor Rd.
Phone: 846-9846
Hours: Monday-Saturday 5:30-10 p.m.
        Sunday 5-9 p.m.
V,P,A,LP,NC,5
Credit cards: Amex/MC/Visa

The word that best describes Margaux's is energy. You will notice it from the minute you walk in. From the sushi bar chefs to the bar staff, wait people, food runners, and of course the kitchen chefs and their support staff, all are moving in full view in what seems to be a choreographed process.

Residing in what used to be a high-end sports store, Margaux's has retained much of the quality decor, the beautiful woodwork, large stone fireplace and 700-gallon fish tank.

The food, however, is the attraction. The menu is basically French-country, but it incorporates many other styles as well. The daily specials number at least 18, varying according to the availability of ingredients. You may find an appetizer such as Sesame Shrimp with Thai Peanut Sauce, or entrees such as Grilled Triggerfish with Lemon and Lime Buerre Blanc, Double-cut Lamb Chops Rolled in Pine Nuts, Feta Cheese, and Fresh Herbs in Puff Pastry. The house menu is more than substantial as well. Chesapeake Bay Crab Cakes with Shrimp and Lemon-basil Butter are always a great start. One might then choose the Roast Rack of Veal Madeira with Wild Mushrooms, or the Steamed Clams, Shrimp and Mussels with garlic, tomatoes and herbs. You will also find an elaborate selection at the fresh shell and sushi bar.

Margaux's has an extensive wine list to enhance any meal. Included, of course, is Chateau Margaux.

The story of how Margaux's came about is almost as intriguing as the food. Co-owners, Steve Horowitz and Richard Hege met by chance while touring the French wine country. Deciding to tour together, they arrived at the legendary Chateau Margaux. A lovely woman showed them around the estate. When she learned they had no lodging, she invited them to stay at the chateau itself. They stayed for many days but never saw their gracious hostess again. It was in her honor that they named their restaurant. Their goal, both say, is to provide their guests with the same delicious meals and generous hospitality they experienced.

Chef Richard is a graduate of the Culinary Institute of America and has owned successful restaurants in New York as well as North Carolina. Chef Scott Cole, whose recipes are included, began his career in San Francisco and has worked in Colorado, Vermont, and Montana.

— recipes shared —
Chilled Salmon Ceviche
Roasted Corn and Sweet Potato Soup
White Lasagna
Asian Mustard Crusted Wild Striped Bass with Ginger Slaw
Potato Crusted Salmon with Tarragon Cream Sauce
Parisian Pan Roast Over Angel Hair Pasta with
Roasted Garlic, Tomato and Saffron Sauce
English Trifle

Margaux's chefs:
Scott Cole,
Richard Hege,
Andrew Pettifer
and Matt
McDonald

71

Chilled Salmon Ceviche

Ceviche is a very appealing appetizer. The colorful ingredients make for a lovely presentation. The fish is uncooked when placed in the marinade and eventually cooks in the acids of the ingredients. Because of this, the texture of the fish is extremely tender. Scott likes to serve his in a fried tortilla shell, or with tortilla chips or water crackers.

Serves 6

2 lb.	salmon diced into 1/4-in. cubes
1	small red onion
2 tsp.	fresh ginger
6	serrano chilies
1/2 cup	tomato (no skin or seeds)
1/2 cup	cilantro, finely chopped
8	limes, juiced
4	lemons, juiced
1/4 cup	vegetable oil
1 tsp.	dry crushed red pepper

• **Procedure**

Dice onions, ginger, chilies and tomatoes. Combine all ingredients and season with salt and pepper. Refrigerate for at least 48 hours. Adjust seasoning again to taste and serve.

• **Wine selection**

Pinot gris can be incredibly harmonious with this dish. The 1992 Reserve from King Estate in Oregon would be a great match. The acidity in the wine, as well as the fruit from an extremely ripe vintage stands up to the salmon. A slight hint of herbaceousness adds a remarkable final touch.

Chef: Scott Cole

Roasted Corn and Sweet Potato Soup

Serves 8-10

5 ears	corn in husk
2 tsp.	fresh thyme
1/2 cup	carrots, diced
3 qt.	chicken stock (canned chicken broth may be substituted if necessary)
1/2 cup	onion, diced
1 cup	sweet potatoes, diced
1/2 cup	celery, diced
	salt and pepper to taste
2 TB	sweet butter

• PROCEDURE

Peel back corn husks, remove silks, and replace husks. Grill corn for 10 minutes. Remove husk and shave kernels. Saute carrots, onion and celery in a little sweet butter. Add thyme and chicken stock. Bring to a boil. Add sweet potatoes, corn and corncobs. Simmer until potatoes are tender. Remove and discard corncobs. Puree half the mixture and add back to remaining mixture. Season to taste with salt and pepper.

Chef: Scott Cole

White Lasagna

This is one of Margaux's most requested items. Preparing it is a lengthy process. Many steps, such as roasting tomatoes and peppers, can be done the day before. Remember to clean the spinach very well and snip off the thick stems.

Serves 6-8

1/2 lb.	lasagna noodles
1 cup	grated mozzarella
12	roma tomatoes
1/2 cup	grated havarti
1 cup	fresh basil leaves, packed and chopped
3	eggs
5 TB	fresh tarragon
2	shallots, chopped
	extra virgin olive oil
2 lb.	uncooked spinach
6 cloves	garlic, chopped
4 TB	butter
1/2 bunch	fresh parsley
2 lb.	shitake mushrooms, sliced
1 qt.	heavy cream
2 cups	ricotta
	salt and pepper to taste
2	eggplants
6	roasted red bell peppers (instructions included)

• **PROCEDURE**

Cook Lasagna noodles per directions until tender. Set aside.

— Cut tomatoes in half lengthwise and set core side up on baking sheet spindle with 1/2 cup basil, 2 TB tarragon, extra virgin olive oil, 2 cloves garlic, fresh parsley, salt and pepper. Bake at 275 degrees for 1 hour. In a large mixing bowl, combine ricotta, mozzarella, havarti, 3 eggs, salt and pepper, 1/2 cup basil, 2 TB tarragon, 3 cloves garlic and 2 shallots.

— Saute spinach in medium-hot pan with 3 TB butter, salt and pepper until wilted. Saute mushrooms in olive oil in a hot pan until tender. Slice eggplant into 1/2-inch rounds and marinate in 5 TB olive oil with 1 clove chopped garlic, 1 TB tarragon, and a pinch of salt and pepper. Roast marinated eggplant in a 500-degree oven about 5 minutes, or until tender. Simmer cream in heavy-bottom saucepan until reduced by half.

— Cool all ingredients completely. Drain all vegetables so that you do not add extra liquid to the lasagna.

• To ASSEMBLE

Use a 9x13-inch pan and layer as follows. Spread 1/2 cup cream sauce in bottom of dish. Cover with layer of noodles. Dot with 1/2 cup cheese mixture, then layer the roasted peppers, the spinach, mushrooms, 1/2 cup cream sauce and a second layer of noodles. Add the remaining cheese, the roasted tomatoes and the remaining cream. Cover and cook for 1 hour at 325 degrees until dish bubbles and cooks through-out.

• ROASTED RED PEPPERS

Broil on a cookie sheet about 4 inches from heat for about 15 minutes. Be careful not to burn. Turn every 3-4 minutes so that all sides puff up. Remove from oven, put peppers in a paper bag and close. Let cool. Remove peppers one at a time. Peel and discard stems and seeds. Canned peppers may be used if necessary.

Chef: Scott Cole

Asian Mustard Crusted Wild Striped Bass with Ginger Slaw

This is a beautiful dish. Almost any white fish, such as perch or catfish, will also work. Scott recommends serving it with steamed asparagus.

Serves 4

Fish:

4	8 oz. wild striped bass fillets
6	eggs
1 lb.	planko (Japanese bread crumbs)
4 oz.	mustard seed
4 oz.	Dijon mustard
6 TB	Coleman's dry mustard
1 1/2 cup	honey
1/2 cup	flour
1 tsp.	white pepper
2 TB	salt

Honey mustard:

4 oz.	Coleman's mustard
6 oz.	honey
2 oz.	water

Gingered slaw:

2	carrots
1	small head cabbage
1 1/2 cup	mayonnaise
4 TB	red wine vinegar
4 TB	white sugar
1	lemon, juiced
1/4 lb.	fresh ginger

• PROCEDURE

Fish:

Remove any bones and all skin from fillets. Combine eggs, honey, Dijon, and dry mustard in a small mixing bowl and whisk until all items are incorporated. Slowly whisk in the flour. In a large mixing bowl, combine bread crumbs and mustard seed with 1 tsp. white pepper and 2 TB salt. Dredge the fillets in the wet mixture first and then in the bread-crumb mixture. On a large plate or cookie sheet, sprinkle a generous amount of the crumbs and place fish on top. Sprinkle a good amount of crumbs over the fish as well. Allow them to sit for at least 1/2 hour. This allows a larger amount of breading to adhere to the fish.

— Over medium heat, and in a large wok or cast iron skillet, warm 1 inch of frying oil. Being very careful, lay fillets gently into the heated grease and allow to cook for 3-4 minutes on each side or until golden brown. Remove from pan and place on paper towels to remove excess grease.

Slaw:

Thinly slice or shred the cabbage. Shred the carrots on a box grater. Place ginger in a food processor and pulse until ginger is broken down into small pieces, then add red wine vinegar and continue to pulse until a paste forms. Remove from the processor and place in a cheese cloth or cloth napkin and squeeze all of the juice out into a bowl and discard the pulp.

— Mix together the juice, mayonnaise, sugar, and lemon juice. Allow to sit for about 15 minutes to allow sugar to dissolve. Mix in carrots and cabbage.

• To Serve

Place the slaw in the center of the plate and slice the fillets in half. Lay them on either side of the slaw and drizzle the honey mustard sauce over. Serve immediately.

Chef: Scott Cole

Potato Crusted Salmon with Tarragon Cream Sauce

This is one of Scott's signature dishes. It is often one of his specials and quite in demand. The instructions sound rather hard, but aren't as difficult as they seem. When you are done, you will have a crispy outside and a very tender piece of fish inside. It is important that the potatoes used have never been refrigerated. This causes them to burn instead of brown when seared. However, the salmon can be prepared ahead of time and refrigerated.

Serves 6

6	7-oz. portions of salmon
	salt and pepper to taste
1	large russet baking potato

Tarragon cream sauce:

2 TB	shallots
2 TB	fresh tarragon
1/4 cup	white wine vinegar
1 cup	reduced veal stock (optional)
1 cup	cream
1/2 cup	dry white wine

• PROCEDURE

Preheat oven to 500 degrees.

— Salt and pepper the fillets. Peel the potato and slice using a mandolin or the slicing side of a box grater. The slices need to be paper thin. With the fillet lying before you horizontally, layer the potatoes across the top of the salmon in a herringbone pattern vertically. Place other slices on the end horizontally overlapping the ends. Turn the salmon over, folding the ends under and continue with the herringbone pattern on the other side, except for the ends. The entire fish should be covered with potato. You should use about 16-18 slices.

— Bring olive oil to a high heat in an oven-proof saute pan. Add the salmon. In the oven, cook on one side for 2-3 minutes until potatoes are golden brown. Turn salmon over and finish cooking another 2-3 minutes.

Sauce:

Combine shallots, tarragon, wine and wine vinegar. Cook over high heat until reduced by 80 percent. Add veal stock. If you do not have this, another cup of heavy cream can be used. Add cream and salt and pepper to taste and serve under the salmon.

Chef: Scott Cole

Parisian Shellfish Pan Roast over Angel Hair Pasta with Roasted Garlic, Tomato, and Saffron Sauce

Serves 6

3	1 1/2 lb. lobsters
2 doz.	clams (thoroughly washed)
2 doz.	mussels (thoroughly washed)
1 doz.	oysters (thoroughly washed)
1 doz.	shrimp
1 lb.	jumbo lump crabmeat
1 doz.	scallops
1 cup	white wine
1 cup	clam juice
1 cup	fish stock (recipe in index)
2	zucchini
2	carrots
2	yellow squash
1 1/2 cups	fennel (diced large)

Sauce:

	shellfish stock (may substitute fish stock or clam juice)
1 cup	garlic cloves (peeled and sliced thickly)
1/2 cup	extra virgin olive oil
4	fillets anchovies (diced)
1 cup	onion, diced
3 cups	plum tomatoes, diced
1 TB	saffron
1/4 cup	fresh basil, chopped
1 TB	fresh thyme
1 tsp.	black pepper
1 tsp.	dry red pepper
1 TB	coarse sea salt

Pasta:

1 lb.	DeCecco capellini pasta

• PROCEDURE

Shellfish:

Steam lobsters, clams, mussels, shrimp, scallops, oysters and fennel in white wine, clam juice, and fish stock until done — about 8 minutes. Remove shellfish and reserve liquid and fennel. Scoop out zucchini,

Parisian Shellfish
Pan Roast

carrots and squash with large end of melon baller. Add vegetables to salted boiling water until done and remove to cold water bath, drain and reserve.

Sauce:
In large sauce pot, heat extra virgin olive oil until very hot. Saute garlic until slightly brown, add onions and caramelize. Add anchovies, tomatoes, reserved shellfish stock, herbs, salt and pepper and saffron. Simmer slowly for 20 minutes. Return shellfish to sauce and prepare to serve.

Pasta:
Cook angel hair pasta in salted boiling water until al dente. Strain and place in 6 large pasta bowls.

• To Assemble
In each bowl over pasta, place 1/2 lobster, 4 clams, 4 mussels, 2 shrimp, 2 scallops, 1 oyster, crabmeat and vegetables. Ladle sauce into bowl. Serve with warm baquettes and sweet butter.

Chef: Richard Hege

English Trifle

This is a very attractive desert. It is best displayed in a glass container so all of the layers are seen.

Serves 6

2	large eggs, separated
1/4 cup	sugar
8 ounces	mascarpone cheese
1 tsp.	almond extract
6	ripe peaches (out of season, canned may be substituted)
1/4 tsp.	cinnamon
2 TB	Myers's dark rum
1/8 tsp.	cream of tartar
1 1/2 cup	fresh blueberries
2 TB	water
1/4 cup	sugar (for blueberries)
30	lady fingers
	creme de cassis

• PROCEDURE

Almond cream:

Place yolks and sugar in a mixing bowl and whip on high for about 5 minutes until thick. Reduce speed to medium and gradually add mascarpone. Whip until smooth then add almond extract. Peel and chop 3 of the peaches and gently fold into the cream.

— Whip the egg whites in a clean, dry bowl on medium until foamy and add cream of tartar. Whip at high speed until soft peaks form. By hand, fold into mascarpone mixture. Refrigerate.

Fruit:

Puree the remaining peaches with the cinnamon and rum. In a medium saucepan, bring blueberries, sugar and water to a slow boil and simmer 15 minutes. Cool before assembling.

• TO ASSEMBLE

Divide peach puree among the glasses. Top that with a thin layer of the mascarpone mixture. Soak the lady fingers with the creme de cassis and make this your next layer, cutting them if necessary. Next divide the blueberry mixture among the glasses and top with a thin layer of the cream. Layer again with lady fingers and top with the remaining cream. Cover and refrigerate at least 4 hours before serving. Garnish with fresh fruit.

Chef: Matt McDonald

PORTOBELLO

Address: 7901-101 Falls of Neuse Rd.
Phone: 847-1790
Hours: Tuesday-Thursday 5:30-10 p.m.
        Friday-Saturday 5:30-10:30 p.m.
        Sunday 5:30-9 p.m.
V,O,N,LP,NC,4
Credit cards: Amex/MC/Visa

Chef Andrew Booger has fond childhood memories of the Portobello Market in London, where he and his family spent many a happy Saturday. He always thought Portobello would be a great name for a restaurant, and when he opened his new restaurant in north Raleigh in 1995, he called it just that.

Andrew attended Strasbourg Culinary Institute in Strasbourg, France, and after returning to London to work for a time, worked in Washington, D.C. at La Nicoise. He then moved to Connecticut, where he met his wife Tara. Tara, who has an associate degree in food service and is co-owner of Portobello, can usually be found taking care of the front of the house while Andrew watches over the back.

Appetizers featured on Portobello's menu may include Fried Portabella Mushroom with Humus and Roasted Garlic Aioli and Pan-fried Rosemary Polenta. Salads may include Hearts of Romaine Salad with Prosciutto and Sweet Onions with Gorgonzola Vinaigrette and Tuscan Bean Salad with Roma Tomatoes, Sweet Onions, Kalamata Olives, Marinated Feta and Lemon Herb Vinaigrette. You may want to try an Orzo Pasta entree with Smoked Chicken and Crimini Mushrooms with a Cashew Scallion Butter, or a Fillet of Beef with Caramelized Shallots and Merlot Jus Lie.

The pizzas are individually hand tossed and stone-fired. Toppings include portabella mushrooms, filet mignon, capers, feta cheese, spinach, artichoke hearts and much more.

Andrew uses vegetable stock in 90 percent of his dishes, creating a light, pure flavor in all.

The restaurant is bistro style, elegant and cozy, divided by a small island bar. Smoking and dining are available on an outside patio.

— recipes shared —
Stuffed Portabella with Smoked Chicken and Creamed Spinach
Saffron Rubbed Grilled Jumbo Scallops
with White Corn and Haricot Vertes Risotto
Lemon, Basil, Lump Crab Cakes with Basil Oil Fried Angel Hair
Seared Tiger Shrimp with Roasted Tomato and
Artichoke Sauce over Romano Crusted Bread
Grilled Rosemary-Garlic Pork Loin with Salad of White Bean,
Pimento, Red Onions and Toasted Almonds

Stuffed Portabella with Smoked Chicken and Creamed Spinach

Advance preparation required.
This is another version of a stuffed portabella. Andrew says you can easily smoke the chicken at home. Soak wood chips for several hours. When grill is ready, drain water from chips and disperse them among the charcoal or stones. Use low heat and close the grill to get a smokier flavor.

Serves 4

4	portabella mushrooms
2	chicken breasts (boneless, skinless, smoked)
1 cup	balsamic vinegar
1 TB	garlic, chopped
1/2 cup	canola or olive oil
	salt and pepper to taste
1 lb.	spinach
1/2 stick	butter
1 cup	sour cream or mascarpone cheese

• PROCEDURE

Remove stems from mushrooms. Clean the mushrooms and marinate them for 1-2 days in balsamic vinegar, 1 TB chopped garlic and oil.

Stuffing:

Preheat oven to 450 degrees.
— Slice smoked chicken breasts into small pieces. Clean spinach and remove stems. Melt butter in a large pan over medium-low heat. Add remaining garlic and cook until lightly brown. Add half of spinach slowly until it wilts. Keep adding spinach until it is completely cooked. When spinach is done, add the chicken. Fold in cheese or sour cream. Stuff the mushrooms with this mixture and place in a pre-heated 450-degree oven for 10-12 minutes.

Chef: Andrew Booger

Saffron Rubbed Grilled Jumbo Scallops with White Corn and Haricot Vertes Risotto

The saffron gives the scallops a wonderfully delicate flavor. Saffron can be found in most gourmet stores. You only need a pinch.

Serves 6-8

2 TB	olive oil
2 lb.	jumbo scallops
1 1/2 cups	risotto rice
6 ears	corn, silked and cut from cob
1 lb.	haricot vertes (or fresh green beans)
pinch	saffron
1 qt.	vegetable or chicken stock
1	medium carrot, diced small
2 stalks	celery, chopped
1	small onion, chopped
1/2 lb.	butter
	salt and pepper to taste

• PROCEDURE

Place the olive oil and scallops in a large bowl. Sprinkle with the saffron and refrigerate.

— Melt the butter and saute the corn, carrots, onion and celery in a large saucepan over medium heat. Sprinkle with salt and pepper. When onions are translucent add the risotto and turn up heat to medium-high. When risotto begins to pop, add 1 quart of the vegetable or chicken stock. Bring this to a boil, stirring constantly to prevent scorching.

— Cut the haricot vertes in halves or quarters and add them to the risotto. Cover and steep until completely stewed.

— Grill the scallops and serve over the risotto.

• WINE SELECTION

With a dish containing a spice so delicate as saffron, the wine should not be too complex, so as not to ruin the whole experience. A wine with rich fruit, firm acidity for the scallops, and just a hint of oak is called for, and Wild Horse Pinot Blanc is just that wine. It's rich fruit, hinting of apple, pairs not only with the saffron and scallops, but with the corn and haricot verte risotto as well.

Chef: Andrew Booger

Lemon, Basil, Lump Crab Cakes with Basil Oil Fried Angel Hair

Advance preparation required.
This is an impressive looking appetizer, with the crab cakes layered over the fried angel hair.

Serves 4-6

3 lb.	lump crabmeat, cleaned
	zest of 1 lemon
2 oz.	lemon juice
8	large basil leaves cut into long thin strips
1/2 lb.	bread crumbs
	salt and pepper to taste
1 lb.	angel hair pasta
1/4 stick	butter

Basil oil:

1/2 lb.	fresh basil leaves
1/4 cup	olive oil
	salt and pepper to taste

• PROCEDURE (one day ahead of serving):

Crab cakes:

Lightly toss crab, lemon zest, lemon juice, basil, bread crumbs, and salt and pepper in a large mixing bowl. If mixture is too dry, add more lemon juice. Make about 6 6-8-oz. oval cakes. Be careful not to make them more than 1-inch thick. Refrigerate for one day.

Basil oil:

Puree basil and oil in a food processor or blender.

Pasta:

Cook pasta al dente according to package directions. Cool in cold water and drain. Toss pasta in a touch of oil. When completely cool, toss in basil oil. Twirl pasta into balls, place on sheet pan and refrigerate uncovered.

• PROCEDURE (for the following day):

Sear the crab cakes in olive oil for 4-6 minutes on each side over medium heat. Remove from pan.

— In same pan, sear pasta on both sides for 5-7 minutes. Add salt and pepper and 1-2 TB freshly squeezed lemon juice.

— To serve, remove pasta and place on serving plates. Put crab cakes over pasta and drizzle pan juice over cakes.

Chef: Andrew Booger

Seared Tiger Shrimp with Roasted Tomato and Artichoke Sauce over Romano Crusted Bread

Serves 6-8

4-6	shrimps per person
	romano cheese, shredded
2 cans	artichoke hearts, quartered
1	loaf french bread (cut in 1 1/2 inch diagonal slices)
1/2 cup	white wine

Sauce:

10	ripe tomatoes, cut in half
4	garlic cloves
6	fresh sage leaves
1	carrot, peeled, cut in rounds
1	small onion, diced medium
2 TB	olive oil
	salt and pepper to taste
	vegetable stock

Basil oil:

1/4 lb.	basil leaves
1/2 cup	olive oil
	salt and pepper

• **PROCEDURE**

Tomato sauce:

Preheat oven to 400 degrees.

— Toss all of the ingredients in a large bowl and transfer to baking sheet, place in oven for 30-45 minutes. Remove and cool. Then purree with enough vegetable stock to create a nice consistency.

Basil oil:

Puree the oil ingredients in a blender or food processor.

Bread and entree:

Preheat oven to 300 degrees.

— Heat a saute pan to medium-high heat, add 1-2 TB olive oil. Baste bread with olive oil and sear in pan.

— Place bread on a baking sheet and sprinkle with shredded romano.

89

Place in oven until cheese is melted.

— Using the same saute pan on medium high heat, sear the shrimp on both sides in a small amount of olive oil. Add artichoke hearts and salt and pepper. When the hearts are warm, deglaze the pan with white wine. Add roasted tomato sauce. Let reduce.

— To serve, remove shrimp from sauce and arrange on bread in a large bowl. Ladle on sauce.

• WINE SELECTION

A complex Merlot would be the best choice for this complex entree. This is the "in" wine of the '90s with its soft tanins and its plum and cherry characteristics. One good choice would be the Franciscan Merlot, Napa 1994.

Chef: Andrew Booger

―――――――――――――

Grilled Rosemary - Garlic Pork Loin with Salad of White Bean, Pimento, Red Onions and Toasted Almonds

Advance preparation required.

Serves 6

Loin:

3 lb.	pork loin
1 TB	chopped garlic
	salt and pepper to taste
1 TB	fresh rosemary
1/4 cup	vegetable or olive oil

Bean salad:

1 lb.	dry white beans
	salt and pepper to taste
1	large red onion
2 TB	sugar
1 bunch	Italian parsley
2	bay leaves
1/2 cup	canned diced pimento
4 oz.	champagne vinegar
1/2 lb.	almonds, slivered

• PROCEDURE

Pork:

Mix garlic, rosemary, salt and pepper with oil, and marinate pork in it for 1-2 days.

Bean salad:

Peel onion and cut in half horizontally. Slice into medium julienne cut. Marinate in the champagne vinegar and sugar, salt and pepper for 1-2 days. Onions will soften and become sweet. Reserve marinade.

— Clean beans and put in a pot with enough water to cover. Cook over medium to low heat for 1 hour. Rinse with cooking water still in the pot to arrest cooling process.

— Preheat oven to 350 degrees.

— Toast almonds in oven until brown, 7-12 minutes.

— Strain water from beans, add pimentos, red onions, and toasted almonds. Add 1/4 bunch chopped parsley and salt and pepper to taste. Add some of the onion marinade. Toss this and let sit for 2-3 hours at room temperature, tossing occasionally.

• GRILL

Grill pork to your liking. If loin is too thick, sear on grill and roast in oven to desired doneness. Serve grilled loin next to bean salad, drizzle a bit of onion marinade over loin.

Chef: Andrew Booger

Grilled Rosemary - Garlic Pork Loin

91

TARTINES

Address: 1110 Navahoe Dr.
Phone: 790-0091
Hours: Monday-Saturday 6-10 p.m.
V,A,S,NC,4
Credit cards: Amex/MC/Visa

Tartines is a quaint restaurant with a bistro atmosphere. You will often find a full house with "just enough room for one more." The clientele is made up largely of returning patrons who enjoy a finely tuned dining experience with linen-clad tables, candles and an enjoyable staff.

Owner and Chef Alain Wellerstein is originally from the south of France. He has grown to love America, but the food he grew up with is still his passion. A reserved man with a warm smile, Alain graduated from the Hotel School of Nice, then trained in London and Switzerland. His continental experience is reflected in his sophisticated menu.

First courses range from Baked Green-lip Mussels with Almond Garlic Butter to Roasted Quail with Bacon Vinaigrette. Entrees include Tournedos of Beef with Cognac Peppercorn Sauce, Roasted Monkfish Tail with Herbs of Provence, Prairie Veal, Calf Sweetbreads, Rack of Lamb, Fillet of Venison and Vegetarian Ravioli. The wine list is carefully chosen to accent the menu with a small concentration of wines from southern France. Reservations are recommended.

— recipes shared —
Roast Duck Breast with Blackberry Sauce
Crabmeat and Goat Cheese Raviolis with Basil Tomato Sauce
Roasted Red Pepper and Tomato Soup

Roast Duck Breast with Blackberry Sauce

This is a delicate winter dish best served with delicate vegetables such as sauteed snow peas and a complementing starch such as sticky rice. As always, the quality of ingredients can make or break a dish so try to use fresh berries when in season. Use duck stock or veal stock recipe in the index. Duck and Goose breasts are traditionally served medium-rare to medium, if you prefer a medium-well breast, add a few minutes to the baking time. Preheat oven to 400 degrees.

Serves 6

    6-8 10-oz. duck breasts

Sauce:
1/2 cup	light brown sugar
4 TB	granulated sugar
2 TB	raspberry vinegar
1 cup	game stock or veal stock
1 TB	butter
3 cups	fresh blackberries (frozen may be substituted)

• PROCEDURE

Duck breasts:
Sear over a medium-high flame for a few minutes skin-side down to melt away the fat. Drain and sear on the other side for 1 minute. Place the breasts skin-side down to bake for 8-10 minutes.

Sauce:
Barely cover the berries with water, bring to a boil, stir in brown sugar and cook for 6-8 minutes. Strain out seeds and puree. In a separate pan heat granulated sugar and vinegar. Simmer for a few minutes and slowly stir in the berry puree and stock. Let this boil for a few minutes. Reduce heat and simmer until the sauce is the consistency of a light syrup. Add butter to sauce before serving.

• WINE SELECTION

In some ways this can be a hard food to pair with wine due to the gamy flavors of the duck and the sweetness of the blackberries, but a nice young Rhone style wine would do the trick. The Bandol from Domain de Tempier would be a wonderful complement to this dish. It has good tannins and earthy qualities to enhance the flavor of the duck, along with enough forward berry fruit to balance out the blackberries. This wine also has just enough soft pepper on the finish to complement the entire dish. Bandol is not an everyday household word but many retail stores will carry the Domain de Tempier due to the quality of this fabulous Rhone producer.

Chef: Alain Wellerstein

Crabmeat and Goat Cheese Raviolis with Basil Tomato Sauce

Raviolis are a traditional appetizer that can be varied in many ways. Use your imagination. It takes a bit of practice to make successful raviolis but the end product is worth it.

Use fresh roma tomatoes in the sauce, if possible. Skin by blanching the tomatoes in boiling water for 20 to 30 seconds until skin begins to welt. Place them directly into cold water. If you can't use fresh tomatoes, canned are okay. This is a great appetizer for the busy entertainer because the raviolis can be made several weeks ahead and frozen. Fresh lump or backfin crabmeat is best.

Serves 4-6

Sauce:

1 cup	tomatoes, peeled and diced
1 cup	crushed tomatoes or canned puree
1/2 cup	white wine
1/2 cup	chicken stock
1 cup	fresh basil leaves
1 tsp.	thyme
1 tsp.	oregano
4	bay leaves
dash	cayenne
pinch	sugar
	salt to taste

Raviolis:

	Eggroll wrappers (cut in fourths) or wonton wrappers
1/2 lb.	Montrachet goat cheese
1/2 lb.	crabmeat
1/4 cup	dry vermouth
1/4 cup	red pepper, chopped
1/4 cup	parsley, chopped
1/2 cup	heavy cream
	salt and pepper to taste

• Procedure

Sauce:

Mix ingredients and simmer 15 minutes. Remove the bay leaves before serving.

Raviolis:

Place all ingredients but wrappers into a food processor and chop finely. Scoop a small amount of filling on the center of a pre-cut square. Wet the edges of another square and place on top. Press the edges lightly. The water will adhere the two pasta layers. Place in boiling water for 3-4 minutes.

• Wine selection

With the combination of crabmeat, goat cheese, and the aromatic herbs reduced in white wine, as well as the acidity from the tomatoes, a good Sancerre is one of the first wines that comes to mind. The acidity and backbone from a sauvignon blanc along with the herbaceous qualities adds a wonderful harmony with the dish. Jean Max Toger produces a wonderful, and relatively easy to fine Sancerre called Cuvee GC. This is a superb wine from a grand cru vineyard that is inexpensive and has tremendous depth of flavor.

Chef: Alain Wellerstein

Roasted Red Pepper and Tomato Soup

This soup can be served hot or cold so it is suitable for summer or winter. It has a fabulous fresh, crisp flavor. To roast the red peppers, place them on a lightly oiled cookie sheet. Roast in a preheated 425-degree oven, turning often. When the skins begin to welt and are almost black, remove from the oven; peel when cool. This process will give the peppers a smoky flavor.

Serves 4-6

4	large red peppers, roasted, peeled and seeded
2 cups	tomatoes, peeled, seeded (canned may be substituted)
1/4 cup	extra virgin olive oil
2	garlic cloves, minced
3 cups	chicken stock
1/2 tsp.	salt
1/4 tsp.	fresh ground pepper
2 TB	balsamic vinegar
1 1/2 TB	fresh chopped basil

• PROCEDURE

Saute garlic in olive oil until tender. Puree the first 7 ingredients in a food processor or blender for about 30 seconds. Simmer for 15 minutes on medium heat. The vinegar and basil is to be added directly before eating. Serve hot or chilled.

Chef: Alain Wellerstein

Tartines owner and chef Alain Wellerstein

VERTIGO

Address: 426 South McDowell St.
Phone: 832-4477
Hours: Lunch: Monday-Friday 11:30 a.m.-2 p.m.
Dinner: Wednesday, Thursday, Sunday 6-10 p.m.
Friday and Saturday 6-10:30 p.m., late menu until 12:30 a.m.
Brunch: Sunday 11 a.m.-2:30 p.m.
V,L,A,C,4
Credit cards: Amex/MC/Visa

Owners Evan Lightner and Susan Goetcheus chose to open their new-generation restaurant in a building that once housed a restaurant of another era, the old Poole's Diner. The space is virtually the same as when Mr. Poole resided. (They even kept the sign intact.) The only changes are small: a knickknack or two, and the works of local artists displayed on the walls.

Don't let the decor fool you. Chef Thor Johnson, a graduate of the Culinary Institute of America, chooses to serve nothing representative of an old-time diner. Chef Matt Steigerwald originally opened Vertigo with Susan and Evan but has since moved to Virginia Beach. He did leave several wonderful recipes to share. Thor meantime continues the challenge of feeding the eclectic crowd of state and town officials during the day, and Raleigh's younger generation in the evenings.

Although the menu changes every few months, here are some samples you may see: starters such as Baked Pecan Goat Cheese Salad with Roasted Red Peppers and Smoked Bacon and Roasted Garlic Dressing, or Sweet Corn and Dixie Beer Battered North Carolina Oysters.

Entrees such as Pan Seared Trout Fillets with Potato Gratin, Grilled Asparagus and Tomato Caper and Garlic Brown Butter, or Grilled Spring Ribeye with Yorkshire Pudding, Gorgonzola, Walnut Butter,

Roasted Parsnips, Brussel Sprouts and Red Wine Jus. Each menu usually varies one or two wonderful vegetarian dishes such as Grilled Balsamic Portabella Mushrooms with Parmesan Risotto Cake, Sauteed Garlic Spinach, Grilled Red Onion and Roasted Red Pepper Vinaigrette. One thing is certain, Vertigo is not just a meal, it's an experience.

— recipes shared —
Braised, Grilled Leeks with Dijon Vinaigrette
Toasted Pumpkin Seed Crab Cakes with Habenero Chili Aioli
Poached Red Snapper with Julienned Vegetables
and Honey-Sage Sauce
Pan Roasted Pork Tenderloin with Apple Ancho Bourbon Sauce

Susan Goetcheus, chef Thor Johnson and Evan Lightner

Braised, Grilled Leeks with Dijon Vinaigrette

This is a delicate and simple appetizer, but very flavorful. Matt suggests to pair this with blanched spring vegetables such as asparagus, fiddlehead ferns or a fresh spinach salad. This also would be a wonderful start to a simple fish entree.

Serves 4-6

4-6	leeks (one large leek per person)
1/4-1/2 cup	dry white wine
	salt and pepper

Vinaigrette:

1	egg yolk
1 TB	Dijon mustard
1/8 cup	white wine vinegar
1	garlic clove
pinch	salt, pepper, sugar
1/4 cup	olive oil

• PROCEDURE

Leeks:

Preheat oven to 400 degrees.

— Cut the dark green ends and root tips off leeks. Quarter leeks lengthwise, clean and drain thoroughly, then place in a single layer in a roasting pan and sprinkle with salt and pepper. Pour in white wine, cover the pan with foil and bake for 25-30 minutes. Drain leeks and grill for 2-3 minutes on each side. Place on a plate alone or over baby Asian greens and drizzle with vinaigrette.

Vinaigrette:

Place all ingredients into a blender and pulse on low speed. Slowly drizzle the olive oil in to the blender until completely emulsified (you may not use all of the olive oil). Add salt and pepper to taste.

Chef: Matthew Steigerwald

Toasted Pumpkin Seed Crab Cakes
with Habenero Chili Aioli

This is a fabulous rendition of traditional crab cakes. The recipe can be increased to become an entree. Use the palm of your hands to form the cakes into an oval shape. Don't squeeze too tightly. Allow them to remain light in texture.

Serves 4-6

1 lb.	backfin crabmeat
1/4 cup	toasted ground pumpkin seeds
2	eggs
1 TB	chili powder
1/4 cup	mixture celery, onions, red pepper, finely diced
1 clove	garlic, diced
1 TB	Dijon mustard
	salt and pepper

Aioli:

1/4 cup	real mayonnaise
1-2 TB	finely chopped garlic
	habenero chili sauce to taste
2 TB	fresh lemon juice

• **PROCEDURE**

Saute vegetables in 1 TB of oil over medium heat until soft, add garlic and saute for 2-3 more minutes. Remove from heat and cool. Mix ingredients for aioli and chill.

— When vegetables are cool, gently mix the remaining crab cake ingredients. Form the cakes into 2-3-oz. portions. Brown cakes in a medium-high skillet with 1-2 TB hot oil. Turn and brown other side. Reduce heat to medium-low, cover pan and cook 4-5 minutes on each side. Drizzle aioli over the cakes or serve on the side for dipping.

Chef: Matthew Steigerwald

Poached Red Snapper
with Julienned Vegetables and Honey-sage Sauce

Serves 4

4   6-8-oz. red snapper fillets

julienne each of the following:
- 1/2 lb.   carrots
- 1   leek (whites only)
- 1   medium zucchini
- 1   medium squash
- 1   medium onion

	fish stock as needed
1/2-3/4 cup	white wine
	salt and pepper to taste
1 tsp.	fresh thyme, chopped
1/4 bunch	fresh sage, thinly sliced
2 TB	honey
1 1/2 TB	whole butter
	oil as needed
	parchment paper (cut to size of pan)

• PROCEDURE

Preheat oven to 350 degrees.
— Heat ovenproof pan (large enough to hold fillets) on high, add oil. Add julienned vegetables and lightly saute. Place snapper fillets on vegetables, keeping them evenly spaced. Add wine and enough fish stock to cover 1/4-1/2 of fillets. Bring to a simmer, cover with oiled parchment and place in oven.
— Cook 8-12 minutes or until done. Remove fillets and distribute vegetables onto four plates. Place fillets on top of vegetables. Reduce poaching liquid by 3/4, add thyme, sage, honey, salt and pepper and bring to simmer. Remove from heat, add butter, stirring until just melted. Pour sauce over fillets and serve.

• WINE SELECTION

A sparkling wine would be a great complement to this dish, one containing a California chardonnay grape such as the Mumm Cuvee Napa Brut, for one example.

Chef: Thor Johnson

Pan Roasted Pork Tenderloin with Apple Ancho Bourbon Sauce

Serves 4

2	2-lb. pork tenderloins
1/4 cup	all purpose flour (seasoned with salt and pepper)
2-4 TB	olive oil
2 TB	shallots, minced
2	Granny Smith apples, peeled, cored and sliced thin
2	dried ancho chilies, reconstituted and sliced thin
3/4 oz.	bourbon
1/4 cup	stock
2 tsp.	fresh thyme, chopped
	salt and pepper to taste
1 TB	butter

• **PROCEDURE**

Preheat oven to 350 degrees.

— Heat ovenproof pan (large enough for both tenderloins), add oil. Dust tenderloins with flour, shake off excess. Sear tenderloins on all sides. Put pan with tenderloins in oven and cook for 10-12 minutes until medium rare. Remove tenderloins from pan and let rest.

— Degrease pan and add thyme and shallots. Saute until soft over medium-high heat. Add ancho chilies and apples and saute. Deglaze pan with bourbon and stock and allow to reduce by about half. Slice tenderloins thinly and fan out onto four plates. Remove sauce from heat and add butter, stirring until melted. Pour sauce equally over tenderloins and serve.

• **WINE SELECTION**

The apple bourbon sauce on this pork is fairly difficult to match but one choice in a pinot noir. As this grape is extremely sensitive to grow, a choice from a cold region is recommended such as the Caneros Creek, Estate Grown Pinot Noir 1995.

Chef: Thor Johnson

WICKEDSMILE

Address: 511 W. Hargett St.
Phone: 828-2223
Hours: Tuesday-Saturday 5:30-10 p.m.
E,V,A,S,NC,5
Credit cards: Amex/MC/Visa

WickedSmile is housed in what used to be a meat packing plant in the '20s. Many of the original beams, bricks and windows add to the nostalgic ambiance, which is occasionally enhanced by the faint rumble and whistle of a passing train.

Chef Paul Fontaine was schooled at Johnson and Wales in Rhode Island and worked in restaurants in Wilmington, Durham, and Raleigh before joining owner Chris Bender at WickedSmile. He recently returned from a work-study program in Chambery, France.

Paul's innovative cuisine includes starters such as Grilled Sweet Potato Ravioli with Gorgonzola and Sesame Creme Fraiche and a Toscana Tart with Summer Tomatoes, Chevre, Roasted Garlic and Sweet Onions. A late-summer menu featured entrees such as Pan Roast of Salmon with Citrus Balsamic Glaze or Hoisin Crusted Rack of Lamb with Candied Ginger, Garlic, Black Beans and Sticky Rice.

— recipes shared —
Panned Breast of Free Range Chicken with Roasted Fingerling
Potatoes and Mushroom Chips with Port Caramel
Baby Mixed Green Salad with Pears, Walnuts and Gorgonzola
Grilled Triggerfish with Tomato Basil Essence
Late Summer Lobster and Sweet Corn Bisque

Panned Breast of
Free Range
Chicken

Panned Breast of Free Range Chicken
with Roasted Fingerling Potatoes
and Mushroom Chips with Port Caramel

Serves 2

2	4-oz. free range chicken breasts
8	fingerling potatoes (may substitute Yukon Gold, cut into wedges)
2	eggs, whisked
1/2 cup	flour
1 cup	fresh bread crumbs mixed with your favorite herbs to taste
	salt and pepper to taste
2 cups	port wine
2 oz.	olive oil
2 oz.	fresh herbs

• PROCEDURE

Rinse the breasts and pat dry. Season with salt and pepper and dust with flour. Dip in the eggs, then in the bread crumbs. The colder the breasts, the more this mixture will adhere during cooking. Saute the breasts in a small skillet with about 1 oz. of the olive oil on medium-high heat until golden brown (about 3-5 minutes on each side). Remove and place in warm oven. In the same pan, saute the potatoes for 5-10 minutes until golden brown and season with salt and pepper. Remove from skillet and reserve in warm oven. Add the rest of the olive oil and saute the mushroom discs until golden brown. When done, remove and pat dry.

Sauce:

Reduce the wine to the consistency of a syrup, being careful not to burn. Allow a few hours for this.

• TO SERVE

Layer the mushroom and potatoes first with the breast on top, drizzle with the sauce.

• WINE SELECTION

Chicken can go with red or white wine, but the richness of the port wine in the caramel sauce in this dish calls for a red. A cabernet sauvignon from Spain, Torres Grand Coronas, is a rich, earthy reserve cabernet made by Migaul Torres that would be incredible with both the chicken and the sauce.

Chef: Jean Paul Fontaine

Chef Jean Paul
Fontaine with owner
Chris Bender

Baby Mixed Green Salad with Pears, Walnuts, and Gorgonzola

A wonderful, simple salad, this makes a great beginning or finale to a meat or chicken entree.

Serves 2

8 oz.	baby mixed greens
2 oz.	walnuts
2 oz.	gorgonzola crumbles
2 oz.	sliced pears
2 oz.	olive oil
1 tsp.	lemon juice
	salt and cracked black pepper

• PROCEDURE

In a bowl, combine lettuce, pears, cheese and walnuts. Mix with olive oil, lemon juice, a pinch of salt and cracked black pepper. Serve in chilled salad bowls.

• WINE SELECTION

This lovely creation would match well with a Riesling from Northern France. A German Riesling, usually juicy and sweet, would not be appropriate. This dish should be paired with a dry wine. Alsatian Rieslings are full-bodied and match nicely to nuts and cheeses. A Hugel Riesling 1989 Alsace would go well.

Chef: Jean Paul Fontaine

Late Summer Lobster and Sweet Corn Bisque

Yields 1 gal.

2 lb.	lobster shells
1 lb.	minced onion
2 oz.	butter
2	cloves garlic, minced
2 oz.	tomato paste
3 oz.	brandy
2 qt.	shellfish veloute (recipe in stocks and sauces section)
2 qt.	heavy cream
1 lb.	lobster chunks
1 lb.	pureed corn kernels
4 oz.	sherry
	salt and pepper to taste

• PROCEDURE

Sweat lobster shells, onions, and garlic in butter for 10 minutes. Add tomato paste, and cook for 10 more minutes. Add brandy and deglaze. Add veloute and simmer for 30 minutes. Strain through cheesecloth and return to pot. Add heavy cream and reduce by 1/4. Add puree of corn, lobster chunks, sherry, salt and pepper. Taste and adjust seasoning.

Chef: Jean Paul Fontaine

Grilled Triggerfish with Tomato Basil Essence

Serves 2

2	8-oz. triggerfish fillets
1 oz.	olive oil
	salt and pepper to taste

Essence:

1 lb.	very ripe plum tomatoes
1 TB	olive oil
	salt and pepper to taste

• **PROCEDURE**

Inspect fish for bones. Season with olive oil, salt and pepper. Grill until fish begins to flake and turns opaque to solid white. Remove immediately, set aside.

Essence:

Preheat oven to 250 degrees.

— Cut tomatoes lengthwise. Oil large sheet pan and sprinkle with salt, place tomatoes cut side down and place in oven for 2 1/2 hours until slightly brown and wrinkled. Place tomatoes in food processor, add pepper and process briefly. Sauce should be thick and chunky. In a bowl, put warm essence on bottom and grilled fish on top. Serve with fresh steamed spinach or asparagus.

• **WINE SELECTION**

The light flavors in this dish should be paired with a Chablis from Northern France. The Domaine Moreau, Fils Chablis Premiere Cru Vaillon 1992 is a lovely match.

Chef: Jean Paul Fontaine

OTHER RALEIGH
RESTAURANTS OF NOTE

CAFE GIORGIOS
Address: 230 Newton Rd.
Phone: 846-9449
Hours: Lunch: Monday-Friday 11:30 a.m.-2:30 p.m.
Dinner: Monday-Friday 5:30-10 p.m.
Saturday 5:30-11 p.m.
E,V,P,A,3
Credit cards: Amex/MC/Visa

EST EST EST TRATTORIA
Address: Corner of Hargett and Salisbury St.
Phone: 832-8899
Hours: Monday-Thursday 11 a.m.-10 p.m.
Friday 11 a.m.-11 p.m.
Saturday 5-11 p.m.
V,A,C,4
Credit cards: Amex/MC/Visa

FOSTERS
Address: 521 Daniels St.
Phone: 832-9815
Hours: Lunch: Monday-Friday 11:30 a.m.-2 p.m.
Dinner: Monday-Thursday 5:30-10 p.m.
Friday-Saturday 5:30-11 p.m.
E,V,O,A,C,3
Credit cards: Amex/MC/Visa

IRREGARDLESS CAFE
Address: 901 W. Morgan St.
Phone: 833-8898
Hours: Lunch: Monday-Friday 11:30 a.m.-2:30 p.m.
Sunday 10 a.m.-2:30 p.m.
Dinner: Monday-Saturday 5:30-10 p.m.
E,V,N,C,3
Credit cards: Amex/MC/Visa

The Museum Cafe

Address: North Carolina Museum of Art, 2110 Blue Ridge Rd.
Phone: 833-3548
Hours: Lunch: Tuesday-Friday 11:30 a.m.-2:30 p.m.
Brunch: Saturday-Sunday 11 a.m.-3 p.m.
Dinner: Friday 5:30-9 p.m.
V,N,D,4
Credit Cards: Amex/MC/Visa

The Rathskeller

Address: 2412 Hillsborough St.
Phone: 821-5342
Hours: Monday-Friday 11:30 a.m.-10:30 p.m.
Saturday-Sunday 12:00-10:30 p.m.
V,N,C,2
Credit Cards: Amex/MC/Visa

Sam's Restaurant and Wine Bar

Address: 3050 Wake Forest Rd.
Phone: 876-4056
Hours: Lunch: Monday-Friday 11:30 a.m.-2 p.m.
Dinner: Monday-Thursday 5:30-10 p.m.
Friday-Saturday 5-10:30 p.m.
E,V,P,A,S,C,4
Credit cards: Amex/MC/Visa

Seasons Restaurant

Grey Stone Shopping Center
Phone: 870-1234
Hours: Monday-Thursday 5:30-9:30 p.m.
Friday-Saturday 6-10 p.m.
V,A,D,4
Credit Cards: Amex/MC/Visa

Swain's Charcoal Steak House

Address: 2816 Millburnie Ave.
Phone: 231-6873
Hours: Sunday 5-9 p.m.
Tuesday-Wednesday 5-9 p.m.
Friday-Saturday 5-10 p.m.
P,A,R,NC,4
Credit cards: Amex/Din/Dis/MC/Visa

WINSTONS GRILLE

Address:6401 Falls of the Neuse Rd.
Phone: 790-1578
Hours: Monday-Thursday 11 a.m.-10 p.m.
Friday 11 a.m.-11 p.m.
Saturday 4:30-11 p.m.
Sunday 10:30 a.m.-10 p.m.
V,P,O,A,S,C,4
Credit Cards: Amex,Din/Dis/MC,Visa

Cary

Restaurants

THE FOX AND HOUND

Address: 107 Edinburgh St. S.
Phone: 380-0080
Hours: Lunch: Monday-Saturday 11:30 a.m.-2 p.m.
Dinner Monday-Saturday 5:30-10 p.m.
E,P,A,S,C,2
Credit cards: Amex/Dis/Din/MC/Visa

The Fox and Hound is the only restaurant in the Triangle offering traditional British cuisine.

Step in the front door and you feel as if you just walked into a pub in England.

This is exactly what the owner, Dane Johnston, wanted to accomplish. He spent quite a bit of time in England and saw that the British treat their pubs as a third home; the first, of course, being the place where they live, the second, church. "The public house in England is a place where life itself takes place for people of all ages and walks of life; politics is debated, advice is sought and found, jobs are offered and lost, births are celebrated, funerals are arranged, romances bloom and fade, and souls are soothed. All social lines are dropped."

The Fox and Hound boasts lovely marble tables, a cherry bar and a stuffed fox. The only brew on tap served is cask-conditioned beer from England, Ireland, or Scotland, although an assortment of bottled beer is available.

On the menu, you will find traditional English starters such as Potato and Smoked Salmon Cakes and Country Pate. Entrees include Bangers and Mash, Mixed Grill of the Midlands, (lamb, pork, and sausage), and Roast Beef and Yorkshire pudding. You will also find an intricate wine selection.

Rabbit Confit over Zucchini Cakes with Fig Relish
Shepherd's Pie
Mint Crusted Grilled Lamb Chops

Rabbit Confit over Zucchini Cakes with Fig Relish

Advance preparation required.
Confit is a traditional way to bake meat, meaning to cook in its own fat. You will often see duck confit on restaurant menus. Obviously it would be hard to obtain enough rabbit fat to bake the rabbit so a substitute has been given.

Serves 4

Rabbit:

4-6	large pieces of rabbit
2 TB	kosher salt
2 tsp.	black pepper
4 cloves	garlic, sliced thin
1 tsp.	ground coriander
1 tsp.	tarragon
1 sprig	fresh rosemary, finely chopped
3/4 cup	vegetable oil
1/4 cup	olive oil

Zucchini cakes:

3	medium zucchini
1/2	onion, finely diced
3	eggs
1/2 cup	flour
	lemon pepper, to taste
	salt and white pepper, to taste

Fig relish:

1 cup	dried black mission figs
2	seedless oranges
dash	cayenne pepper
dash	ground cumin
dash	ground cinnamon
	salt and white pepper, to taste

Rabbit:
Make a mixture of the salt, pepper, garlic, coriander, tarragon, and rosemary. Generously coat each peice of the rabbit with the mixture and
cure overnight. The next day, sear the rabbit in hot oil and place in a
roasting pan. Cover completely in the vegetable and olive oil. Cover
with foil and cook in 300-degree oven until the meat falls off the bone.
About 2 to 2 1/2 hours. Let cool in fat and remove to store.

Cakes:
Grate zucchini, only the outer surface; do not expose the seeds. Place
all ingredients except salt and white pepper in a large mixing bowl and
combine. Divide the mixture into quarters. In a medium pan with a touch
of oil from the rabbit, fry until golden brown and repeat on the other
side. Add the salt and pepper just before cooking.

Fig relish:
Skin oranges and cut planks off the outer sides, leaving the centers.
Finely dice planks, squeeze juice out of centers and reserve. Slice figs
into 1/8-inch medallions. Place figs, diced oranges and reserved juice
into mixing bowl. Season with spices, salt and pepper.

• Tᴏ sᴇʀᴠᴇ
Put zucchini cakes on bottom, rabbit pieces on top and dollop relish
between the rabbit.

Chef: Dane Johnston

Shepherd's Pie

Serves 4-6

1-1/4 lb.	ground lamb
1	onion, finely diced
1 1/2	carrot, finely diced
1/2 cup	mushrooms, sliced
1/4 cup	tomato paste
1/4 cup	flour
2 cup	beef stock (or canned beef broth)
2 tsp.	salt
2 tsp.	black pepper
1 tsp.	thyme
1 tsp.	rosemary
4 cups	mashed potatoes

• PROCEDURE

Sear lamb in a hot pan with no oil. When partially cooked, drain excess fat. Add onions, carrots, and mushrooms and stir to incorporate. Add tomato paste. Cook for several minutes. Add flour and mix well, allowing any liquid to absorb the flour. Add stock 1 cup at a time. Bring to a simmer before adding any more. Cook until carrots are done, about 20 minutes. Serve in a large bowl over mashed potatoes.

Chef: Dane Johnston

Mint Crusted Grilled Lamb Chops

The Fox and Hound recommends serving this dish with roasted red potatoes and a blanched vegetable such as green beans or asparagus. Dane accompanies this dish with a fruit chutney.

Serves 4

12	lamb chops
2 TB	olive oil
2 TB	garlic, minced
1 TB	rosemary
	lemon pepper to taste

Crust:

2 cups	bread crumbs
1/2 cups	melted butter
1 bunch	fresh mint, chopped
1 TB	green peppercorns, crushed and ground
	salt and white pepper, to taste
	Dijon mustard

• Procedure

Marinate lamb chops in olive oil, garlic, rosemary, and lemon pepper for 2 or more hours. Mix all ingredients for crust except mustard.
— Grill the chops to your liking. Coat one side of the chops with the Dijon mustard. Top with the crust. Place under broiler until browned and serve.

Chef: Dane Johnston

MAXIMILLIANS

Address: 1284 Buck Jones Rd.
Phone: 460-6299
Hours: Lunch: Tuesday-Friday 11:30 a.m.-2 p.m.
          Dinner: Tuesday-Saturday 6 p.m.- (varies, call)
V,N,LP,C,5
Credit cards: Amex/MC/Visa

Maximillians was one of the first high-caliber restaurants in Cary. Because of that and Chef Michael Schiffer's interesting combinations of spices and brothy sauces, it became an instant success.

This restaurant, which seats only 36, is one of few of its type that has a take-out menu.

All of the entrees are served with soup or salad. The menu changes often, but some items you may find are Thai Barbecue Duck, Spice-Crusted Ribeye, Roast-Herb-Crusted Pork Loin, Grilled Oak Island Scallops, Mixed Grill of Seafood or Pan Seared Sesame Red Snapper. Grilled pizzas are also offered on a regular basis.

All this is quite a change from Schiffer's early days. He started out with an ice cream shop in New England. His customers wanted food as well as ice cream, and he began making soups and gradually moved up to a other items. He still loves ice cream, though, makes it himself and includes one of his recipes here.

— recipes shared —
Grilled Flat Bread with Black Olive Tapenade
Red Chili Scallops with Spicy Ginger Shrimp Sauce
Kona Coffee Ice Cream with Hazelnut Truffle

Maximillians owner
and chef Michael
Schiffer with Gayle
A. White

Grilled Flat Bread with Black Olive Tapenade

Advance preparation required.

Yields 1 large loaf

Focaccia dough:

3/4 package	dry yeast
1/2 cup	warm water
2 cups	unbleached all-purpose flour
1/2 cup	cold water
1 1/2 TB	olive oil
pinch	sugar
3/4 TB	salt

Tapenade:

pitted Kalamata olives
extra virgin olive oil
garlic
fresh sage
fresh oregano
roasted red peppers
arugula
black pepper
capers
gorgonzola cheese
crushed red peppers

• PROCEDURE

Prepare dough one day ahead. Mix yeast in warm water and let stand for 15 minutes in mixer bowl. Place flour in mixer bowl. Combine cold water, olive oil, sugar, salt in a separate bowl and pour into mixer bowl. Mix with dough hook until dough forms. Knead until smooth on floured board. Let stand for 15 minutes, then refrigerate.

— Remove dough from refrigerator 1 hour before baking and let sit at room temperature for one hour.

— Heat oven to 500 degrees. Flatten dough by stretching gently (be careful not to tear) until it reaches about 10 inches in diameter. Let sit for 10 minutes, while chopping capers, roasted red peppers, olives, herbs, garlic until medium fine. Place in bowl with 3 TB olive oil. Add black pepper. Spread mixture over focaccia. Sprinkle on gorgonzola to taste. Bake on preheated pizza tile until golden brown and cheese has melted. Garnish with arugula.

Chef: Michael Schiffer

Red Chili Scallops with
Spicy Ginger Shrimp Sauce

Serves 4

Ginger shrimp sauce:

2 TB	shallots, chopped
1 TB	garlic
1 TB	ginger
	star anise
1-2	smoked chipotle chilies
	sweet chili sauce to taste (available in oriental markets)
pinch	cumin
1	red bell pepper, diced
8	shiitake mushrooms
2 oz.	white wine
6 oz.	chicken stock
2 oz.	coconut milk
1/2 cup	baby shrimp (raw)

Red chili scallops:

5	large scallops per person
1/2 cup	olive oil
3	large guajillo chili pods
2 tsp.	cumin
1 tsp.	powdered garlic
1 tsp.	black pepper
1 tsp.	salt
1 tsp.	fennel seed
	cilantro

• PROCEDURE

Sauce:

Sear 2 TB shallots in olive oil. Lower heat, add ginger and garlic and saute for one minute. Add red bell pepper, scallions, shiitakes and saute for another minute. Deglaze with 2 oz. of white wine. Add pinch of cumin, smoked chopped chili, 1 piece star anise. Wait until 1/2 of the liquid is reduced and add 6 oz. chicken stock, 2 oz. coconut milk, and sweet chili sauce to taste. Add 1/2 cup shrimp once sauce has reached desired consistency. Let simmer for 2 minutes.

Red Chili Scallops with Spicy Ginger Shrimp Sauce

Scallops:

Finely grind chili pods and fennel seeds in spice mill and add other spices. Place scallops in a large bowl with 1/2 cup olive oil. Sprinkle on spice mixture and toss. Grill scallops over high heat, turning every 2 minutes until interior just begins to lose translucency (6-8 minutes). Place over pasta with finely chopped cilantro. Pour on ginger shrimp sauce.

• WINE SELECTION

The intensity of spice in this dish calls for a sweeter wine, such as a German Mosel Reisling. A good spatlese from most producers would work well. Selbach-Oster is a fabulous producer.

Chef: Michael Schiffer

Kona Coffee Ice Cream with Hazelnut Truffle

Serves 3

4 cups	half and half
10	egg yolks
3/4 cup	sugar
1 cup	milk
1 1/2 cup	Frangelico
1 lb.	kona coffee beans
1/2 lb.	semi sweet chocolate
1/4 lb.	toasted hazelnuts, coarsely chopped

• PROCEDURE

Bring half and half to a slow simmer and add coffee beans. Continue a slow simmer for 25 minutes or until desired strength. Strain and discard coffee beans. Return to heat. Whisk 1/2 cup sugar with egg yolks. Add 1/2 of cream mixture to eggs while vigorously stirring. Add egg and cream mixture to the rest of the half and half. Heat on low setting until mixture starts to thicken. Strain through fine mesh and refrigerate 24 hours. Add Frangelico and sugar to taste. Freeze in ice cream machine according to directions.

— Melt semi-sweet chocolate in sauce pan over low heat with hazelnuts. Spread melted mixture on buttered cookie sheet. Let cool in refrigerator until hard. Chop into bite-size pieces once hardened. Mix into coffee ice cream and return to freezer.

Chef: Micheal Schiffer

SORRENTO

Address: Triangle Factory Shops, 1001 Airport Blvd.
Phone: 380-0990
Hours: Monday-Friday 11:30 a.m.-10 p.m.
Saturday 12-10 p.m.
Lunch until 4 p.m.
V,P,N,S,NC,3
Credit cards: Amex/MC/Visa

You will find movers and shakers from the Research Triangle Park as well as hungry shoppers dining at Sorrento's. The restaurant is simple yet elegant, bright and open during the day, cozy and romantic at night.

Chef Scott Pigeon was nine when his mother began bringing him to help out in the family restaurant in New Jersey. He began peeling carrots and potatoes. By 14, he was doing many other jobs. He held positions ranging from kitchen manager to head chef at several restaurants before moving to Raleigh to be sous chef at Claudios.

Among the entrees at Sorrento are Cappallini with Shrimp in Pink Brandy Cream Sauce, Veal Parmingana (Milanese or Picatta), and Chicken Marsala or Franchese.

— recipes shared —
Veal Scaloppine a la Romano
Grilled Prawns with Three-Pepper Sauce
Linguini with Green-lip Mussels and Littleneck Clams
Raspberry Sorbet

126

Veal Scaloppine a la Romano

Serves 4

12 oz.	scaloppinis of veal
1 cup	romano cheese, grated
1 cup	broccoli florets
1 cup	all purpose flour
3	eggs
1 cup	shiitake mushrooms
3 oz.	Marsala wine
3 oz.	extra virgin olive oil
3 tsp.	lightly salted butter
2 cups	veal or beef stock
3 tsp.	chopped shallots
	salt, pepper, garlic powder to taste

• PROCEDURE

Coat veal with flour, dip in beaten eggs and dredge in grated cheese, being careful not to create clumps on the meat. Place pan on medium-high heat. When pan is hot, pour in olive oil and saute veal on both sides for 1-2 minutes or until golden brown. Remove from pan, set aside.

— Using the same pan, pour out oil and replace with butter. When butter has melted, saute the shallots. When soft, add the mushrooms and broccoli. Saute until shallots are translucent and mushrooms are soft.

— Deglaze pan with Marsala wine. Add veal stock, season to taste and let reduce by half. Replace veal, cook for a few more minutes to heat, and serve.

• WINE SELECTION

A traditional Italian dish demands a traditional Italian wine, a great chianti—in particular the 1990 Chianti Classico from Fontodi, a truly remarkable wine. A certain dustiness is definitely a plus with this wine, which also has a ripe, rich, raisiny fruit that is complex without being overpowering.

Chef: Scott Pigeon

Grilled Prawns with Three-Pepper Sauce

This is an attractive and colorful appetizer. Served over baby greens it becomes a wonderful salad.

Serves 4

12	large shrimp, size U-10 (10 to the lb.)
4	red bell peppers
3 oz.	basil
2 tsp.	chopped garlic
4	poblano peppers
3	banana peppers
4 oz.	white wine
2 oz.	olive oil
4 oz.	lightly salted butter
	salt, pepper, garlic powder to taste

• PROCEDURE

Grill shrimp evenly on both sides. This will take 1-2 minutes.
— In a hot pan on medium-high heat, add olive oil and saute garlic until golden brown. Add peppers and saute for 1-2 minutes, then add basil. Deglaze pan with white wine and season to taste. Add butter and shrimp. Serve alone or over a bed of baby greens.

Chef: Scott Pigeon

Linguini with Green-lip Mussels and Littleneck Clams

This dish calls for some hard-to-find ingredients, but for a special occasion it is well worth the search.

Serves 4

12	green-lip or New Zealand mussels
12	littleneck clams
8 oz.	clams, minced
2 cups	red bell pepper, julienned
2 cups	pepper, julienned
8 TB	Spanish onion, diced
1 cup	pancetta or bacon, chopped
4 tsp.	lemon juice
	basil, oregano, salt and pepper to taste
1 tsp.	worcestershire
6 cups	clam juice
4 TB	garlic, chopped
	linguini for four

• **PROCEDURE**

In a large saute pan on medium-high heat, saute garlic in a bit of olive oil until golden. Add onions and pancetta, saute for a few minutes and drain most of the fat.

— Add mussels, clams, peppers, minced clams, wine, worcestershire, lemon and clam juice. Season to taste. Cover and cook for approximately 10 minutes.

— Cook the linguini according to directions for al dente. Toss the pasta with a bit of the juice from the clams. To serve, place pasta in a large bowl and pour ingredients over pasta, carefully distributing the clams and mussels evenly between bowls.

Chef: Scott Pigeon

Raspberry Sorbet

This is an attractive non-fat desert often served between courses to cleanse the palate. Other berries may be substituted, such as blackberries, strawberries or blueberries. Almond cookies are a great accompaniment to any sorbet.

Serves 4

2 cups	water
1 cup	granulated sugar
4 cups	raspberries
2/3 cups	black currant liqueur
4 TB	fresh lemon juice
2	egg whites
	fresh mint

• PROCEDURE

Combine water and sugar in a saute pan and bring to a boil for 1-2 minutes. Let cool to room temperature. Add raspberries, lemon juice and liqueur to the sugar mixture. Let sit for about an hour.

— Strain mixture through a fine strainer to make sure all seeds are removed. Taste the mixture, and add more lemon juice or sugar to taste.

— Place mixture in a small storage container and freeze overnight. Mixture will not freeze completely.

— Remove from freezer and place in a food processor with the egg whites and blend for 30 seconds. Re-freeze and serve.

Chef: Scott Pigeon

Durham

Restaurants

MAGNOLIA GRILL

Address: 1002 9th St.
Phone: 286-3609
Hours: Monday-Thursday 6-9:30 p.m.
Friday 6-10 p.m.
Saturday 5:30-10 p.m.
V,A,S,D,4
Credit cards: MC/Visa

When it comes to Triangle dining, Ben and Karen Barker are precedent setters. They have received national recognition and won many honors, including the coveted James Beard Award. They continue to uphold the tough standards set in 1986 when Magnolia Grill first opened.

Ben and Karen both are graduates of the Culinary Institute of America. They met on the first day of class and did their externship together in Cape Cod before getting married.

Ben's love for food is more a lifestyle than a learned process, having grown up with aunt and grandmother who fed the family directly from it's farm. They cured their own ham, made fresh bread daily, and were always canning and preserving.

Karen, from Brooklyn, was a history major at college but discovered she loved cooking more.

Ben continues to place a global spin on the local flavors he was raised with. He says you will always find pork on his menu and this he smokes himself. Other examples on the ever-changing menu are Leeks and Fennel Chowder with Grilled Chicken, Saffron Rice and Red Pepper Rouge or Warm Salad of Asparagus, Fingerling Potatoes & Choggian with Organic Arugula Topped with Apple-smoked Bacon Vinaigrette. Entrees may be Pecan Crusted Halibut in a Corn and Field Pea Vinaigrette, or Grilled Spring Chicken with Caramelized Vidalia

Onion Jus. And after dinner you might choose a Banana Brown Betty with Gingersnap Crumbles and Caramel Ice Cream, or a Warm Chocolate Lava Cake with Whipped Creme.

Magnolia's wine list is extensive and artfully selected by Ben himself to accompany the current menu.

— recipes shared —
Cream of Vidalia Onion Soup
Carolina Grits Souffle
Pickled Shrimp with Crab and Pepper Slaw and
Smoked Tomato Remoulade
Brown Sugar Pear Poundcake

Ben and Karen Barker

133

Cream of Vidalia
Onion Soup

Cream of Vidalia Onion Soup

Serves 8

4 oz.	smoked country bacon, julienned
1/2 cup	unsalted butter
3 lb.	Vidalia onions, thinly sliced (may substitute other sweet onions)
8 cloves	garlic, peeled, left whole
2 cups	dry white wine
1 qt.	chicken stock (preferably homemade)
1	bay leaf
1 TB	fresh thyme (or 1 tsp. dried)
1 cup	creme fraiche or sour cream
	salt, fresh ground white pepper, Tabasco and nutmeg to taste
2 cups	homemade croutons
1 bunch	chives, snipped

• PROCEDURE

In a large Dutch oven, cook bacon slowly until crisp. Remove to paper towels and reserve. Add butter, onions and garlic to bacon renderings, cover and cook over low heat, stirring often until onions are translucent and lightly caramelized. Add wine, stock, bay leaf, and thyme. Bring to boil and simmer 30 minutes.

— Remove bay leaf and puree soup in food processor or blender, in batches if necessary. Pass soup through the fine blade of a food mill (optional). Chill. Whisk in cream and creme fraiche or sour cream. Season with salt, white pepper, Tabasco and nutmeg. Serve in chilled bowls. Garnish with reserved bacon, croutons and chives.

• WINE SELECTION
Chardonnay, especially a rich and buttery one, always works well with Vidalia onions. Talbott Chardonnay from Monterey is the epitome of such a wine. The richness of fruit and the acidity in this wine go well with the cream in the soup, with just a bit of toasty oak for the bacon in the dish. It is the butteriness, though that so enhances this dish, making the Vidalias stand out with a sort of creamy sweetness. For a little lighter style of chardonnay, Talbott makes a "second wine" named Logan that would also work with this dish.

Chef: Ben Barker

Carolina Grits Souffle

Serves 8

2 cups	homemade chicken stock
1 cup	water (or may use total of 3 cups water instead of combination)
2 tsp.	kosher salt
1 cup	half and half
1 cup	white grits (preferably stoneground, definitely not instant)
5	eggs, separated
4 TB	unsalted butter
1 1/2 cups	white or yellow sharp cheddar, grated
1/4 cup	roasted garlic puree (or 1 TB minced fresh garlic)
1/2 cup	scallions, sliced thin crosswise
	coarsely ground black pepper, kosher salt and Tabasco to taste

• PROCEDURE
Butter a 2-qt. casserole or souffle dish. In a 3-qt. heavy-bottom saucepan, bring stock, water, half and half and salt to boil. Stir in grits, reduce heat to medium and cook, stirring often until thick, smooth and

135

creamy. Beat egg yolks. Temper with a spoonful of hot grits and stir into grits. Stir in cheese, garlic puree, butter, salt, pepper and Tabasco to taste. Cool at room temperature.

— One hour before serving, preheat oven to 375 degrees. In a stainless steel bowl, beat egg whites to a stiff peak. Gently fold egg whites and scallions into grits mixture and spoon into buttered souffle dish. Bake 30-40 minutes until grits set. (If the surface appears to be browning too much, cover with foil until set.)

Chef: Ben Barker

Pickled Shrimp with Crab & Pepper Slaw and Smoked Tomato Remoulade

Serves 10, as appetizer

Pickled shrimp:

2 lb.	medium shrimp (31-35 count), cooked, then shelled and deveined
1	medium Vidalia or Bermuda onion, sliced paper-thin
2	lemons, sliced thin and seeded
1-2	dried cayenne peppers, broken into pieces
1/2 cup	capers, drained
6 cloves	garlic, peeled
4	bay leaves

Marinade:

1 cup	white wine vinegar or tarragon vinegar
1/2 cup	water
1/4 cup	whole coriander seeds
1 TB	mustard seed
1 TB	fennel seed
1 tsp.	allspice berries
4 slices	fresh ginger
	salt to taste
	1 cup olive oil

• PROCEDURE

Shrimp:

In 2 qt. jars, pack shrimp, onion, lemon, garlic, and bay leaves in alternating layers. Divide marinade between jars, seal and refrigerate 24 hours or up to one week, turning jars upside down frequently to distribute marinade. Keep refrigerated.

Marinade:

Combine vinegar, water and spices in a non-reactive pan. Bring to boil and simmer 10 minutes. Season to taste with salt, cool and add olive oil.

CRAB AND PEPPER SLAW

1/2	medium green cabbage (Savoy or early Jersey preferred), cored and julienned
1	sweet red pepper, seeded and julienned
1	sweet yellow pepper, seeded and julienned
1	green bell pepper, seeded and julienned
2	carrots, peeled and grated
1 lb.	lump crabmeat, picked
1 cup	smoked tomato remoulade (recipe follows)
	lemon juice, salt and pepper as needed

• PROCEDURE

Combine cabbage, peppers, and carrots in stainless bowl. Add remoulade and fold to combine. Adjust seasoning; should have decent acid to counterbalance sweetness of vegetables and crabmeat. Gently fold in crabmeat so as not to break up lumps. Refrigerate 1 hour for flavors to meld.

SMOKED TOMATO REMOULADE

1/2 cup	tarragon wine vinegar
1 cup	white wine
3	shallots, minced
2	egg yolks at room temperature
1 cup	olive oil
1/4 cup	smoked tomato puree, or more to taste
2 TB	roasted garlic puree
1/4 cup	finely diced cornichons
1/4 cup	chopped capers
2 TB	chopped fresh tarragon
2 TB	chopped flat-leaf parsley
1 tsp.	Tabasco, or more to taste
	lemon juice, salt and pepper to taste

• PROCEDURE

Combine shallots, vinegar, and wine in a non-reactive saucepan. Bring to boil, then reduce to simmer. Cook until reduced to 1/4 cup. Cool.

— In blender or food processor, combine wine reduction, roasted garlic puree, egg yolks, and tomato puree. Pulse to combine. With machine running, add oil in a fine stream to emulsify. Transfer to stainless bowl.

— Fold in capers, cornichons, and herbs. Season to taste with Tabasco, salt, pepper and more smoked tomato puree if desired. Adjust acidity with fresh lemon juice.

• TO SERVE

Place a mound of slaw in center of each plate or large service platter. Surround with pickled shrimp. Drizzle with remaining remoulade as desired. Garnish with flat-leaf parsley.

Chef: Ben Barker

———————————

Brown Sugar Pear Poundcake

Karen says this cake can be made several days ahead of time and is best served lightly toasted with vanilla ice cream. When this is served at Magnolia Grill, a pear compote is added and the dessert is drizzled with a bit of caramel.

Yields 1 10-inch bundt or tube cake

3 1/2	cups flour
1 1/2 tsp.	baking powder
1/2 tsp.	salt
12 oz.	butter (room temperature)
1 TB	vanilla extract
1/2 tsp.	nutmeg
1 lb. +1/4 c.	light brown sugar
5	eggs
3/4 cup	milk
1/4 cup	pear brandy, plain brandy or orange juice
2 1/4 cups	ripe but firm pears, peeled and diced 1/4-inch

Glaze:

    1/3 cup   sugar
    1/3 cup   pear brandy, plain brandy or orange juice

• PROCEDURE

Preheat oven to 350 degrees.

— Thoroughly butter pan. Line with flour, shaking out excess. Set pan aside. Sift flour, salt and baking powder together. Reserve. Cream butter with vanilla extract and nutmeg, very gradually adding brown sugar until the mixture is smooth and light. Add eggs 1 at a time, mixing just enough to incorporate each addition. Add reserved flour-baking powder mixture alternately with milk and pear brandy, stopping occasionally to scrape the bowl thoroughly. Stir in diced pears. Place batter in prepared pan. Bake for approximately 1 hour and 25 minutes. Cake will be golden brown, firm to the touch, just starting to pull away from the sides of the pan, and will test done with a cake tester.

— Cool in pan for 10 minutes. Meanwhile, combine sugar and pear brandy over low heat until mixture comes to a simmer and sugar dissolves. Turn cake out of pan. Apply warm glaze over the entire surface with a pastry brush. Allow to cool.

Chef: Karen Barker

NANA'S

Address: 2514 University Dr.
Phone: 493-8545
Hours: Monday-Saturday 5:30-10 p.m.
V,A,S,NC,4
Credit cards: Amex/MC/Visa

Nana's was an instant success when Scott Howell opened it in December, 1992, and it has never lost momentum. It has been featured in many national magazines and was deemed the number one restaurant in the country by *Esquire* in 1993.

Scott, who is from Asheville, was a business major in college, then attended the Culinary Institute of America in New York. He worked under renowned chef David Bouley in New York before moving on to work at restaurants in southern California and Imolia, Italy. He returned to North Carolina to work with Ben Barker at Magnolia Grill.

Nana's is an elegant little place with eclectic art created by Stephen Silverleaf displayed throughout. Although the tables wear linen, the restaurant has a casual feel. One of the secrets of its success is the communication between Scott and his guests. He often delivers his creations directly to the table, and diners with special dietary needs may find him personally taking their orders to ensure every detail.

The menu rotates about two times weekly and features some of our area's most exotic ingredients. Starters may include Carpaccio of Roasted Portabella with Crispy Fennel and a White Truffle Oil, or Grilled Mountain Trout over Red Oak Leaf Greens with Walnut Blackberry Vinaigrette.

Entrees may be Grilled Manchester Quail over Organic Barley and Roasted Fennel in a Blackberry Sauce, or Roast Pork Loin over Wilted Mustard Greens and Sweet Potato Gratin with Porcini Mushroom Sauce.

The wine list reflects Scott's love of Italian wines and the bar is one of the only cigar-friendly bars in the Triangle.

— recipes shared —
Traditional Southern Pork Barbecue
Caramelized Onion Risotto with Corn and Bacon
Blackberry Polenta Bread Pudding
Spicy Pecan Ice Cream

Nana's Scott Howell

Traditional Southern Pork Barbecue

Although this dish takes very little time to prepare, advance preparation is required and will add to the quality. The sauce is best made three days in advance. The pork should be marinated for at least two days, but three days is better.

Serves 8-10

Sauce:

1/3 cup	honey
1/3 cup	molasses
1 head	garlic, broken into cloves, unpeeled
2 TB	whole cumin seeds
1 TB	whole black peppercorns
8	dried chilies
2	bay leaves
3 TB	tomato paste
48 oz.	whole, canned tomatoes, peeled
1 qt.	white vinegar
4 cups	water
1/4 cup	salt

Pork:

2	boneless pork butts (about 3 lb. each)
10-12	hamburger buns

• PROCEDURE

Sauce:

Combine honey, molasses, garlic, cumin, coriander, peppercorns chilies and bay leaves in a large pot over medium heat. Cook uncovered for 30 minutes, stirring occasionally. The mixture will become thick and aromatic and the garlic brown. Add tomato paste and tomatoes and cook for 10-15 minutes, stirring frequently to break up tomatoes. Add vinegar, water, and salt. Sauce will be thin. Simmer uncovered for 2-4 hours, stirring occasionally.

— Reserve half of the sauce to marinate pork. Remove any garlic peel from remaining sauce and let cool. Puree in blender or food processor. The sauce will remain thin.

Pork:

Marinate pork in enough sauce to cover entirely. Cover container and refrigerate for 2 days. At the end of the first day, turn the pork in the marinade.

— Grill the pork over a slow fire (about 200 degrees), fat side up. Cover grill and let it sit for about 3 hours, then baste about every 30 minutes with remaining sauce. After 4 hours, turn the pork over and cook for another 2 hours. (For oven roasting use the same procedure with a roasting rack in a 200-degree oven.) Remove the pork and let sit until cool enough to handle.

— Pull the pork apart with your hands or slice across the grain in 1/2-inch slices. Chop pork coarsely and place in a large bowl. Add remaining marinade and toss to coat.

• To SERVE

Place a generous amount of pulled or sliced pork on a bun, drizzle some sauce on top. Serve extra warmed sauce on the side.

Chef: Scott Howell

Caramelized Onion Risotto with Corn and Bacon

This risotto can be served on its own or as a sidedish. You can reduce the fat by altering the amount of bacon, if you choose. To prepare corn for roasting or grilling, pull back the husks and remove the silks. Replace husks and soak briefly.

Serves 4

3	medium ears silver queen corn
7 TB	unsalted butter
3	large Vidalia or other sweet onion
4 oz.	bacon cut into 1/4 inch strips
8 cups	chicken stock
1	medium onion, chopped
1	carrot, chopped
1	celery rib, chopped
2 cups	arborio rice
1 cup	white wine
1/4 cup	freshly grated parmesan cheese
	salt and pepper to taste
	fresh chervil sprigs for garnish

• PROCEDURE

Preheat oven to 350 degrees, or prepare grill.

— Grill or roast corn for about 15 minutes, turning occasionally, until kernels are tender. Let cool slightly, then remove husks and cut off kernels into a bowl. Set aside and reserve cobs.

— Melt 3 TB of butter in a large non-reactive saucepan. Add sliced Vidalia onion and cook over high heat stirring constantly, until caramelized—about 25 minutes. Add to the corn kernels. Add bacon to saucepan and cook over high heat, stirring until brown and crisp—about 3 minutes. Transfer to paper towels to drain. Pour off all but 2 TB of fat.

— In another large saucepan, bring corn cobs and chicken stock to a boil and keep warm.

— Heat bacon fat. Finely chop onion, carrot and celery in a food processor. Add to bacon fat and cook over medium-high heat until soft, stirring constantly (about 3 minutes). Add rice to same pan and stir until rice is evenly coated with fat. Add white wine and stir constantly until almost all the liquid has been absorbed, about 2 minutes. Stir in corn, Vidalia onions and bacon.

— Add 1 cup of chicken stock to rice and cook over medium heat, stirring constantly until absorbed. Continue to add stock gradually, stirring constantly until all stock is absorbed. Cook until rice is tender—about 25 minutes. Stir in remaining 4 TB of butter and parmesan cheese, season with salt and pepper. If rice is sticky, add more stock.

Caramelized
Onion Risotto with
Corn and Bacon

Place on plates and garnish with chervil sprigs.

• **Wine selection**
Depending on what risotto is paired with, it can be complemented with almost any wine. In this case the caramelized onions and bacon are elements that stand up to many reds. A good dolcetto, such as the 1994 Gaja Dolcetto Creme, would be perfect.This wine comes from one of the best producers in Italy and is very consistent from vintage to vintage. It has a velvety forward fruit, with just enough good Italian earthiness, to be a match for the caramelized onions.

Chef: Scott Howell

Blackberry Polenta Bread Pudding

Scott often serves this over a lemon curd sauce. The berries can be blueberries or blackberries. Polenta can be made a day before serving. If so, cover and store at room temperature.

Serves 4-6

Polenta:

3/4 cup	all-purpose flour
2/3 cup	yellow cornmeal
1 TB	baking powder
	pinch of salt
2 sticks	softened unsalted butter
1 c. + 1 TB	sugar
4	large eggs, separated
2	large egg yolks

Custard:

1	vanilla bean, split
4 cups	heavy cream
10	large egg yolks
1 cup	sugar
1 pt.	fresh blackberries plus extra berries for garnish

Polenta:

Preheat oven to 325 degrees.

— Grease a 9x5-inch loaf pan. In a bowl, combine the flour, cornmeal, baking powder and salt. In another bowl, cream the butter with the sugar until light and fluffy. Beat in the 6 egg yolks in 3 batches. Fold in dry ingredients in 3 batches until just mixed. Do not overmix.

— In a separate bowl, beat the egg whites until firm but not dry. Stir 1/3 of egg whites into the batter, then fold in the remaining whites. Spread the batter in the prepared pan and bake for about 45-50 minutes until a cake tester comes out clean. Cool in pan on a wire rack.

Custard:

In a medium saucepan, scrape seeds from vanilla bean into the heavy cream, then add the bean. Bring to a simmer over medium-high heat. In a separate bowl, whisk egg yolks with sugar. Slowly whisk in the hot cream mixture. Strain mixture into a bowl and let cool. Stir in berries.

— Grease a 9x13-inch baking pan. Cut polenta into 1/2-inch slices and spread out on a cookie sheet. Toast in the oven (still at 325 degrees) for about 7 minutes, or until lightly browned. Let cool.

— Tear toasted polenta into 3/4-inch-thick strips and spread in greased baking pan. Pour custard over the polenta, evenly distributing berries. Set dish in a larger pan and add enough hot water to the second pan to reach halfway up the sides of the pan with polenta in it. Cover the polenta/custard mix and bake it for about 2 hours. Let cool slightly. Serve pudding garnished with fresh berries.

Chef: Scott Howell

Spicy Pecan Ice Cream

Pecans are a tradition in the South and cayenne may be a surprising ingredient, but crossing culinary boundaries often creates pleasant surprises. This ice cream is a prime example.

Serves 4-6

1/2	vanilla bean, split
1 1/2 cups	heavy cream
1/2 cup	half and half
5	large egg yolks
3/4	cup sugar
2 TB	dark rum
4 TB	unsalted butter
2 oz.	pecan halves
1/4 tsp.	cayenne pepper
	pinch of salt

• PROCEDURE

In a saucepan, scrape seeds from vanilla bean into the heavy cream and half and half, then add the bean. Bring to a simmer over medium-high heat. Whisk egg yolks in a separate bowl with 1/2 cup sugar. Slowly add hot cream, whisking constantly until mixture will coat the back of a spoon (about 5 minutes). Strain into a bowl and let cool, then stir in rum.

— In a small pan over medium-high heat, melt the remaining sugar and heat until golden brown (about 5 minutes). Stir in butter and pecan halves and cook until pecans are completely coated, stirring constantly. Spread nuts in a pan or plate and let cool. Sprinkle with salt and cayenne pepper.

— Break pecans into small pieces and stir into custard. Freeze custard in an ice cream maker according to manufacturer's directions. Serve alone or as an accompaniment to cake or cookies.

Chef: Scott Howell

POP'S

Address: 810 West Peabody St.
Phone: 919-956-7677
Hours: Lunch: Monday-Friday 11:30 a.m.-2:30 p.m.
**   Dinner: Monday-Friday 5:30-10 p.m.**
**   Saturday 5:30-11:15 p.m.**
**   Sunday 5:30-9 p.m.**
V,N,C,2
Credit cards: Amex/MC/Visa

Bon Appetit named Pop's one of the country's top new restaurants in 1996—and no wonder. It is owned by Ben and Karen Barker of the Magnolia Grill and Scott Howell of Nana's.

Situated in a renovated tobacco warehouse, Pop's has extremely high ceilings and a full-view kitchen with a wood-burning pizza oven, where Chef Brack May presides.

Brack started working in restaurants in the San Francisco Bay area when he was 14. After college, he moved to Santa Monica and worked in the film industry before turning back to restaurants. He attended the New England Culinary Institute and cooked in restaurants in California and Florida before coming to North Carolina to take the top job at Pop's, where his rustic Italian cuisine has proved highly popular.

The menu at Pop's is apt to feature starters such as the "Big Bowl" of mussels with sausage in white wine, garlic, and chili flakes, or Basil Gnocchi's with Pancetta, Oven-dried Tomatoes and Olive Pesto. For entrees you may choose a pizza or calzone with such fillings as chicken confit, caramelized onions, and smoked mozzarella or a linguini with clams, smoked bacon, grilled corn, and sweet pickled jalapenos. Other choices include Goat Cheese Ravioli with Roasted Mushrooms, Spinach, and Tomatoes, or Grilled Ribeye with Warm Pepper Relish.

Grilled Ricotta Salata Salad with Caponata Bruschetta
Pistachio Crusted Goat Cheese Salad
with Roasted Corn Dressing
Roasted Vegetable Salad with Raspberry Balsamic Vinaigrette
Marinated Pork Chops with Grilled Polenta
and Sun-dried Plum Sauce
Cornmeal Ricotta Poundcake with
Mascarpone Cream and Apricot Compote

Grilled Ricotta Salata Salad
with Caponata Bruschetta

Serves 6

1 lb.	wedge of ricotta salata (mild solid sheep's milk cheese)
2 cups	caponata (recipe to follow)
6	1/2 bias slices of baguette
3 cups	baby salad greens

Caponata:

1/4 cup	soaked golden raisins
1	zucchini
1	red onion
1	tomato, diced
1	yellow squash
1/2	eggplant
1	red pepper
3 TB	balsamic vinegar
2 TB	olive oil
1/2 tsp.	red pepper flakes
1/4 cup	chopped parsley
1 TB	brown sugar
	salt and pepper to taste

• **PROCEDURE**

Slice the cheese into three equal wedges, then slice each wedge in half. Oil and sprinkle with pepper. Set aside for grilling later.

Caponata:

Slice the squash, zucchini, eggplant and red onions into about 3/8-in.

Grilled Ricotta
Salata Salad

slices for grilling. Cut the red pepper in quarters for grilling. Grill all of the vegetables except tomatoes until well scored and set aside. Saute the tomatoes in olive oil for 2 minutes, add vinegar and cook for 4-5 minutes on medium heat. Add remainder of ingredients and cook until warm. The mixture should have a sweet and sour flavor. Cool and re-serve.

• To Assemble
Place a small nest of the baby greens on the plates and sprinkle with a touch of oil, vinegar and lemon juice. Place about 3 TB of the caponata on each piece of grilled bread and lean against the baby greens. Grill the cheese for about 2 minutes, just until marked and warm. Stand the cheese against the bruschetta and serve immediately.

• Wine selection
The chef suggests a 1994 Cakebread Sauvignon Blanc, or a 1994 Jermann Pinot Grigio.

Chef: Brack May

Pistachio Crusted Goat Cheese Salad with Roasted Corn Dressing

Serves 6

1	12-oz. log of your favorite goat cheese (cut into 6 equal parts)
30 spears	blanched asparagus
8-10 cups	mixed baby greens
2 cups	roasted pistachios (roast raw nuts for 10 minutes at 350 degrees)
2 cups	peanut or canola oil for frying the goat cheese
1 1/4 cup	Japanese breadcrumbs
1 tsp.	salt
1/2	tsp. pepper
2 eggs	whisked with 2 TB water
2 cups	seasoned flour

Dressing:

3	ears corn, roasted or grilled
2	eggs
4 tsp.	minced garlic
3 tsp.	honey
1 tsp.	salt
1 cup	olive oil
1/2 tsp.	pepper
2 tsp.	cider vinegar

• PROCEDURE

Place the pistachios, breadcrumbs, salt and pepper in a food processor and pulse until the nuts are in about 1/8-inch chunks. Form the pieces of cheese into a patty and dip into the egg and water mixture, then into the seasoned flour, back into the eggs and into the nut mixture, pressing it into the cheese. When done, place in the refrigerator for 15-20 minutes to set.

Dressing:

Puree all of the dressing ingredients in a blender except for the oil. Slowly stream in the oil to emulsify.

• TO ASSEMBLE

While oil is heating for the goat cheese, assemble the salad by placing the asparagus on the plate pointing from the inside of the plate outward like sunrays. Toss the greens in the vinaigrette and place about 1-1 1/2 cups in the middle of each plate. Pan fry the goat cheese patties until golden and place in the center of the salad. Drizzle a bit of the vinaigrette around the plate and serve immediately.

• WINE SELECTION
This dish is difficult to match with any wine, but try Domaine Richou Anjou, Rouge 1994.
— The chef also suggests 1993 Lewis "Reserve" Napa Chardonnay.

Chef: Brack May

Roasted Vegetable Salad with Raspberry Balsamic Vinaigrette

This is an elegant, colorful salad that can be served on it's own, or Brack likes to serve it with the marinated pork dish that follows this recipe.

Serves 6

1 bunch	asparagus
3	carrots cut in 1-inch half moons
2	medium red onions sliced
2	medium yellow squash cut in 1-inch cubes
2	red peppers cut in 1-inch squares

Vinaigrette:

2 tsp.	Dijon mustard
	freshly ground pepper to taste
2 TB	balsamic vinegar
1 1/2 TB	raspberry preserves
1/2 tsp.	kosher salt
4 TB	raspberry vinegar
1/4 cup	walnut oil (or substitute other oil)

• PROCEDURE
Vinaigrette:
Whisk all ingredients together and refrigerate until needed.

Vegetables:
Blanch the asparagus for about 4 minutes and shock with ice water to stop cooking process. Roll all vegetables in olive oil, 3 TB chopped shallots, salt and pepper. Roast the vegetables at 350 degrees for 18-20 minutes. Cool and save for salad. Place the vegetables in an organized fashion on a salad plate and drizzle with the vinaigrette.

Chef: Brack May

Marinated Pork Chops with Grilled Polenta and Sun-dried Plum Sauce

To save time, you can make polenta a day ahead.

Serves 6

6	8 oz. pork rib chops

Polenta:

4 TB	olive oil
1 cup	whole milk
2 cups	cornmeal (polenta grade, coarse)
1/4 cup	mixed herbs (parsley, oregano, basil)
6 cups	water
3 tsp.	kosher salt
1/2 stick	butter
2 oz.	parmesan cheese

Marinade:

	juice of 2 oranges
1/2 cup	parsley
	salt and pepper to taste
1/4 cup	olive oil

Plum sauce:
- 1 cup   prunes
- 2 cups   chicken stock (or 3 cups canned chicken broth and 1 cup canned vegetable broth reduce on stove by half)
- 1 cup   Marsala wine

• PROCEDURE

Polenta:
Butter a 9x12-inch pan. Bring water and milk to a boil. Add olive oil and salt and slowly stream in the polenta cornmeal until all is added. Stir constantly until the polenta begins to pull from the sides (about 20 minutes). Pour directly into the pan and cover with waxed paper. Refrigerate until needed.

Pork:
Rub marinade on chops and let set for at least 15 minutes.

Sauce:
Soak prunes in the Marsala for at least one hour. Strain and add the stock, heating mixture on the stove.

• TO ASSEMBLE
Grill the chops on a pre-heated grill for 5-6 minutes per side and remove. Cut the polenta into squares and oil them before grilling 2 minutes per side. Place the polenta on the plate and the pork over half of the polenta. Drizzle the plum sauce over the pork.

• WINE SELECTION
One wine stands out for this dish—Crozes-Hermitage Domaine Thalabert from Paul Jabaulet Aine. A lighter style than a Hermitage yet with many of the same intrinsic qualities, this great Rhone wine seems to intensify the flavors of the pork. And the richness of the Syrah grape withstands the acidity of the balsamic vinegar.
— The chef also suggests 1993 Matanzas Creek Merlot.

Chef: Brack May

Cornmeal Ricotta
Poundcake

Cornmeal Ricotta Poundcake with Mascarpone Cream and Apricot Compote

Yields 1 large poundcake

Poundcake:

1 lb.	butter
6	eggs
1 1/3 cups	ricotta cheese
2 1/2 cups	cake flour
1 cup	cornmeal
3 cups	sugar
2 tsp.	vanilla
1/2 tsp.	salt
1/2 tsp.	baking soda
1/4 cup	buttermilk

Mascarpone cream:

1/2 cup	whipped cream
1/2 cup	mascarpone cheese

Dried apricot compote:

2 cups	dried apricots (cut in half)
1 cup	sugar
	zest and juice of 1 small orange
1 cup	golden raisins
1 cup	sweet Marsala wine

Cake:
Preheat oven to 350 degrees.

— Lightly butter bundt pan. Cream butter and sugar together until light and fluffy. Add eggs one at a time, mixing well between. By hand, fold in the vanilla and ricotta cheese. Sift all of the dry ingredients together and gently fold into mixture. Add the buttermilk last. Bake until inserted knife comes out clean.

Mascarpone cream:
After whipping cream, gentle fold in the mascarpone cheese.

Dried apricot compote:
Combine fruits and cover with water, refrigerate overnight. Drain liquid into a pan and add sugar. Simmer until sugar is dissolved. Add fruit, Marsala, zest and juice. Cover and cook for 15 minutes until tender. Serve at room temperature.

• To SERVE
Dollop compote in center and drizzle cream along the edge.

• WINE SELECTION
The chef suggests 1993 Rivetti Moscato D'Asti "La Spinetta."

Chef: Heather Terhune

OTHER DURHAM
RESTAURANTS OF NOTE

FISHMONGERS
Address: 806 W. Main St.
Phone: 682-0128
Hours: Tuesday-Friday 11:30 a.m.-2 p.m.
Monday-Friday 5-9:30 p.m.
Saturday 12-9:30 p.m.
Sun 12:30-9 p.m.
A,C,2
Credit cards: Amex/MC

FRANCESCA'S DESSERT CAFE
(Desserts only)
Address:706 B. Ninth St.
Phone: 286-4177
Hours: Sun-Thur 10 a.m.-11:30 p.m.
N,C,
Credit cards: MC/Visa

NINTH STREET BAKERY
Vegetarian
Address: 776 Ninth St.
Phone: 286-0303
Hours: Monday-Thursday 7 a.m.-6 p.m.
Friday 7 a.m.-11 p.m.
Saturday 8 a.m.-11 p.m.
V,O
Credit cards: MC/Visa

PAPA'S GRILL
Address: 1821 Hillandale Rd.
Phone: 383-8502
Hours: Monday-Friday 11:30 a.m.-2:30 p.m.
Monday-Thursday 5-10 p.m.
Friday-Saturday 5-10:30 p.m.
V,P,N
Credit cards: Amex/Dis/Din/MC/Visa

PARIZADE

Address: 2200 W. Main St.
Phone: 286-9712
Hours: Monday-Friday 11:30 a.m.-2:30 p.m.
**   Monday-Thursday 5:30-10 p.m.**
**   Friday-Saturday 5:30-11 p.m.**
**   Sunday 5:30-9 p.m.**
V,L,S,O
Credit cards: Amex/Car/Din/Dis/MC/Visa

TAVERNA NIKOS

Address: Brightleaf Square
Phone: 682-0043
Hours: Monday-Saturday 11 a.m.-3 p.m.
**   Monday-Saturday 5-10 p.m.**
S,N,3
Credit cards: Amex/Din/MC/Visa

WASHINGTON DUKE INN

Address: 301 Cameron Blvd.
Phone: 490-0999
Hours: Breakfast: Monday-Sunday 7-10:30 a.m.
**   Lunch: Monday-Sunday 11:30 a.m.-2:30 p.m.**
**   Dinner: Monday-Sunday 5:30-10 p.m.**
E,O,N,5
Credit cards: Amex/Car/Din/MC/Visa

Chapel Hill

Restaurants

AURORA

Address: Historic Carr Mill
Phone: 942-2400
Hours: Lunch: Monday-Friday 11:30 a.m.-2 p.m.
Dinner: Nightly 6-10 p.m.
V,N,S,NC,4
Credit cards: Amex/MC/Visa

Aurora has been a mainstay in Carrboro for nearly 20 years and has remained virtually unchanged, serving fresh northern Italian cuisine, including the only hand-rolled pasta in the area. Not only is the pasta made from scratch but so are the bread, rolls and breadsticks.

Aurora's planked floor, lace-laden windows and partial brick walls bearing local art help to create its ambience.

The food is art as well. "Gwen won't tell you this herself," says owner Hank Strauss, "but she has an infinite talent for food. Everything she touches is a success."

Chef Gwen Higgens was raised in Pennsylvania and attended college at the University of North Carolina. Her mother died when she was young, and as soon as she was old enough to bring a stool to the stove, she began cooking. She's been at it ever since. Cheerful and passionate about her work, Gwen is dedicated to maintaining Aurora's consistent high quality.

I suggest starting your meal at Aurora with a minestrone or antipasti, then precede your entree with a primo pratto such as Cappella d'Angelo con Pesto e Gambretti (fresh shrimp grilled and served over homemade citrus angel hair pasta with lemon, garlic, basil and pine nuts topped with fresh romano). Follow with an entree such as Marinated Lamb grilled to medium-rare with garlic-flavored lamb bordelaise on herbed northern white beans and roasted potatoes, or Salmon con Salsa d'Pinot Grigio Capperi (soy-marinated salmon seared and served with a garlic infused Pinot Grigio sauce with capers and Dijon mustard). There are an abundance of wines to choose from as well as elegant desserts.

— recipes shared —
Halibut with Crab and Pancetta Hash and Grapefruit Vinaigrette
Linguini with Sun-dried Tomato Pesto and Roasted Vegetables
Caramel Ice Cream

Halibut with Crab and Pancetta Hash and Grapefruit Vinaigrette

Crispy pancetta and flavorful hash make this a wonderful fish entree.

Serves 4

4	halibut fillets
3 oz.	pancetta
1 cup	seasoned flour

Hash:

2 TB	shallots
2 TB	garlic
2	baking potatoes, shredded and liquid squeezed out
1 cup	napa cabbage, finely chopped
1 cup	shiitake mushrooms, sliced
1 cup	carrots, grated
	salt and pepper to taste
1 cup	backfin crabmeat

Vinaigrette:

2	small red onions
1	whole grapefruit, juiced
1 TB	balsamic vinegar
6 oz.	pancetta
1/4 cup	olive oil
2 tsp.	lemon juice
	salt and pepper to taste

• Procedure

Saute pancetta over medium-high heat until crispy and remove from pan. Add grapefruit juice, lemon juice, vinegar and olive oil from vinaigrette ingredients. Whisk to incorporate. Grill onions in thick slices on both sides. Separate and add to vinaigrette. Set aside.

— Preheat oven to 350 degrees.

— Dredge fish in seasoned flour and sear in 1 TB olive oil on each side until lightly browned. Finish off in preheated oven for 8-15 minutes or until desired doneness.

— In 1 TB oil saute the ingredients for hash over medium high heat. When vegetables are slightly soft, add crabmeat. Squeeze lemon over pan. Place hash on plate, place fish over hash. Pour vinaigrette over fish and hash and garnish with crispy pancetta slices. Serve at once.

• Wine selection

An elegant white burgundy from France would stand up to both the vinaigrette and the pancetta hash quite well. A good choice would be Domaine Matrot Mersault 1995.

Chef: Gwen Higgens

Halibut with
Crab and
Pancetta Hash
and Grapefruit
Vinaigrette

Linguini with Sun-dried Tomato Pesto and Roasted Vegetables

This is a tasty vegetarian dish. Incorporate more of your favorite vegetables if desired. Gwen suggests using a hearty pasta such as linguini or fettucini.

Serves 4

Pesto:

3 oz.	soaked sun-dried tomatoes
2 oz.	pimento
2 cloves	garlic, peeled
2 TB	pine nuts
2 TB	parsley, chopped
1/2 cup	fresh basil leaves
2 TB	parmesan cheese
1 cup	olive oil
	salt and pepper to taste

Linguini:

1	medium zucchini, (sliced lengthwise 1/2-in. thick)
3	medium shiitake mushrooms, sliced
2	roma tomatoes, sliced lengthwise
bunch	asparagus
	chopped garlic
	linguini to serve 4

• PROCEDURE
Pesto:
Combine all ingredients in a food processor or blender and grind until mealy. Do not overprocess.

Entree:
Preheat oven to 450 degrees.
— Cook pasta and set aside.
— Place zucchini, mushrooms and roma tomatoes in single layer in a large, oiled sheet pan. Sprinkle with salt and pepper and chopped garlic to taste. Roast for 20 minutes. Coat the asparagus with a bit of olive oil, add to other vegetables and continue roasting about 10-15 minutes or until vegetables begin to brown.

163

— To serve, toss 2 TB pesto with each serving of linguini and top with roasted vegetables.

• WINE SELECTION

This Italian pasta classic with its tangy pesto calls for an older, subtle Barbaresco from Piedmonte Italy. Try the Bruno Giaso Barbaresco 1989.

Chef: Gwen Higgens

Seated are chef Gwen Higgins and owner Hank Strauss with Aurora staff on back row

Caramel Ice Cream

This recipe requires an ice cream maker. The ice cream has a terrific rich flavor, a result of roasting the white chocolate.

Serves 4-6

1 lb.	white chocolate (do not use almond bark)
2 TB	dark creme de cocoa
1/2 TB	almond extract
1 TB	vanilla
2 cups	cream
2 cups	light custard (recipe to follow)

Light custard:

2 cups	milk
1/2	vanilla bean
3/4 cup	milk
	pinch salt

• PROCEDURE

Custard:
Cook all ingredients in double boiler until liquid will coat the surface of a spoon.

Ice cream:
Preheat oven to 300 degrees.
— Bake white chocolate for at least 40 minutes and as long as 1 1/2 hours, stirring every 20 minutes to brown evenly. The darker the chocolate becomes, the richer the flavor. Do not allow it to become black.
— Mix cream into caramelized chocolate while still hot. Let cool and remove lumps. Strain and add remaining ingredients. When cool, freeze according to your ice cream maker instructions.

Chef: Gwen Higgens

CROOK'S CORNER

Address: 610 W. Franklin St.
Phone: 919-929-7643
Hours: Dinner: Monday-Sunday 6-10:30 p.m.
       Sunday brunch: 10:30 a.m.-2 p.m.
V,O,N,D,S,C,2
Credit cards: Amex/MC/Visa

Crook's Corner opened in 1949 as a fish and produce stand, but the owner, Rachel Crooks, was mysteriously murdered two years later. The building changed hands many times after that, serving as taxi stand, gas station, and barbeque house. In 1982, Gene Hamer and the legendary chef Bill Neal opened it as a fine-dining restaurant.

Neal, who died in 1991, established Crook's philosophy of serving creative Southern fare using only fresh ingredients, bought locally when possible. These standards are successfully upheld by the current chef, Bill Smith, who began his career at La Residence in 1979.

Although his professional background is in French cuisine, Bill is no stranger to Southern fare. He was born and raised in New Bern and has fond memories of his great-grandmother's big noontime spreads of country cooking. "It was a huge deal and delicious," he recalls. "In our family good cooking was always treasured."

The menus Bill prepares at Crook's change daily, but they feature such items as Country Ham and Vegetable Soup, Miami Spice (an appetizer of cold boiled shrimp, served with hot pepper sorbet), and main courses such as Cajun Ribeye, Yellow Squash Pie, and Old Fashioned Barbeque. Constants on the menu include the popular Hoppin' John, and Shrimp and Grits.

This is often on Crook's menu and is very popular. The green Tabasco creates an attractive color on the chicken when baked and is not nearly as hot as you might expect.

You can also add other ingredients to stuff the chicken, if you choose, such as hot peppers or onions. Bill suggests serving it with mashed potatoes or potato salad and, of course, fresh vegetables.

Serves 4-6

2	**whole fresh chickens**
1+ bottles	**Green Tabasco**
2	**whole lemons**
2	**garlic cloves**
	fresh herbs of your choice (thyme, rosemary, sage, lemon thyme or parsley)
1 cup	**chicken stock (or canned chicken broth)**
1/2 cup	**white wine**

• **PROCEDURE**

Preheat oven to 400 degrees.

— Clean and dry the chickens and place them on a rack. Salt and pepper the inside and stuff each with 1 lemon, a clove of garlic and fresh herbs. Truss the chicken with spiral skewer or old-fashioned needle and string. Douse the chickens with 1/2 bottle each of the Tabasco and sprinkle with salt and pepper. Place in the oven, uncovered, and immediately reduce the heat to 350 degrees.

— When the chicken begins to sizzle, baste for the first time. Baste every 20-25 minutes using the chicken stock. On the last baste before serving add a bit more Tabasco.

— Bake the chicken to an internal temperature of 190 degrees, being careful not to touch the bone when testing. Or bake about 20 minutes per pound and check to see that the juice from the chicken is running clear. Remove the chickens and the rack from the pan and deglaze the pan with white wine. Strain the liquid and pour over the chicken on the serving dish. Also pour over mashed potatoes if you are including them.

Chef: Bill Smith

This appetizer is a favorite at Crook's. It can be very attractive if colorful red and yellow tomatoes are used. In the cornmeal you can add any ingredient you prefer, such as fresh roasted corn, diced hot peppers and fresh herbs.

Serves 6-8

2-4	tomatoes (thinly sliced, horizontally)
1 cup	yellow or white cornmeal
4	beaten eggs
1/2 cup	cheese, grated (use your favorite)
3 1/4 cups	water, boiling
1 tsp.	salt
1/2 cup	cottage cheese (rinsed and drained)
	parmesan cheese to finish

Fresh Tomato and Polenta Tart

• PROCEDURE

Grease 9-inch pie pan or spring form pan before you begin. In a heavy pan, bring the water to a boil and slowly drizzle in the cornmeal and salt, stirring constantly until it pulls away from the edges of the pot. Remove the pan and slowly mix the eggs into the hot mixture, stirring constantly. Add the cottage cheese, grated cheese and any herbs you choose.

— Immediately place the cornmeal mixture into the prepared pan pressing it evenly around. Place the tomatoes on the tart in a circle working from the outside in, or in a fan pattern, again working from the outside in, alternating red and yellow if you are using both. Sprinkle with salt and pepper.

— Allow the tart to set for 10 minutes before baking. Bake for about 10 minutes at 350 degrees. Sprinkle with parmesan cheese, bake until cheese is melted, and serve immediately.

Chef: Bill Smith

Honeysuckle Sorbet

Honeysuckle Sorbet

This is truly a unique dish created by Bill with a little encouragement from owner Gene Hamer. Crook's has many honeysuckle vines, which give off a heavenly aroma during early summer evenings on the outdoor dining patio. Many times Gene would comment on the sweet smell and ask Bill if there was anything he could create from the blossoms. Bill came up with this scrumptious sorbet.

Serves 2

1 cup	honeysuckle-infused water
1 cup	sugar
pinch	cinnamon
squirt	fresh lemon

Honeysuckle-infused water:

3 cups	fresh honeysuckle blossoms
4 cups	cool water

• PROCEDURE

Honeysuckle-infused water:

Pick honeysuckles at night when they are most aromatic. Rinse them gently in cool water, not cold or warm. Place them in a plastic container in 4 cups of cool water, cover loosely with plastic wrap and leave on the counter overnight. Do not refrigerate. In the morning, gently mash the blossoms in the water and strain. Keep the water and discard the flowers.

Sorbet:

In a saucepan, heat the sugar with a bit of infused water to make a syrup. When the sugar has completely melted, remove from stove and stir in the rest of the infused water, cinnamon and lemon. Make in your ice cream maker according to manufacturer's directions.

Chef: Bill Smith

FEARRINGTON HOUSE

Address: 2000 Fearrington Village Center
Phone: 542-2121
Hours: Saturday 6-9 p.m.
Sunday 6-8 p.m.
V,P,O,N,S,D,7
Credit cards: Amex/MC/Visa

Fearrington House Restaurant is in the 1927 Fearrington family home, a maze of charming dining rooms that used to bustle with family life. Each room has it's own style, with antiques and original artwork, making for a true country inn dining experience.

Chef Corey Mattson, an avid outdoorsman, hunter and world traveler, has been at Fearrington for 10 years, and has been at the forefront of expanding our area's culinary boundaries. He often speaks of how difficult it was to obtain unusual, even fresh, ingredients as recently as five years ago. Now distributors are learning to cater to these demands, he says, leading to more creative cooking.

As testament to Corey's skill, Fearrington House boasts the only AAA Five Diamond Award in the state.

The restaurant offers a pre-fix four-course meal that changes seasonally. You may find as a first course Air Cured Antelope Carpaccio with fresh mozzarella, basil, and tomato, dressed with balsamic vinegar and olive oil, or Braised Quail Medallions in a country-ham gravy with potato croutons. Between courses, a salad or sorbet is served, then you are on to a main dish that may include Roasted Boneless Leg of Rabbit with Pancetta, Fresh Herb Spatzel and Rabbit Stock Reduction, or Grilled Beef Tenderloin on Parmesan Disks with Three Peppercorn Sauce and Wild Chive Mashed Potatoes. You may also find veal, fish, pork tenderloin, game bird, antelope or venison. Corey is always sure to have a vegetarian entree as well.

After dinner you will have a choice of delectable desserts made by pastry chef Heather Mendenhall whose talents are celebrated by Corey. You might find the popular Hot Chocolate Soufflé, Vanilla Bean Creme Brulee, Frozen Malted Milk,and Banana Parfait (a combination of banana pistachio cake and pistachio sauce).

— recipes Shared —
Corn Bread with Smoked Tomato Sauce
Rice Paper Wrapped Tuna with Ginger Sauce
Softshell Crayfish over Cheese Grits
Mixed Grill of Quail, Lamb, and Veal with Waffle-cut Potatoes
and Balsamic Vinaigrette
Sauteed Halibut over Roasted Fennel with Red Pepper
and Kalamata Olive Tapenade
Oven Roasted Plum Strudel with Port Wine Ice Cream
Frozen B-52 Parfait

Corn Bread with Smoked Tomato Sauce

This is one of Corey's favorite recipes, a versatile dish that can be served as a whole meal or an accompaniment to any Southern dish.

Serves 8-10

Cornbread:

1 1/2 cups	flour
1 1/2 cups	cornmeal
1 TB	freshly cracked black pepper
1 1/2 TB	baking powder
4	eggs
1 3/4 cups	milk
1/2 cup	shortening (melted)
1/4 cup	honey
1 can	white sweet corn
1 lb.	cooked smoked sausage
6 oz.	shredded sharp cheddar cheese
1	small red onion, minced
1	small apple, diced small

Tomato sauce:

10 lb.	ripe tomatoes, peeled, with seeds and juice removed
	soy sauce to taste
1 clove	garlic, minced
5 cloves	shallots, minced
1 cup	olive oil
1 TB	thyme
1 tsp.	rosemary
1	bay leaf
1 tsp.	black pepper
	kosher salt to taste
	sugar to taste
	heavy cream to taste

• PROCEDURE

Corn bread:

Preheat oven to 425 degrees.

— Combine flour, cornmeal, pepper, salt, and baking powder in a large mixing bowl. In a separate bowl, thoroughly mix eggs, milk, shortening and honey. When mixed, add to dry mixture. Fold in sweet corn, smoked sausage, cheddar cheese, red onion and apple. Bake for 20-25 minutes in a greased sheet pan. Internal temperature should reach 190 degrees. Cool before cutting.

Tomato sauce:

Spray tomatoes lightly with soy sauce and smoke over wood chips as you would a piece of fish. In a large pot sweat garlic and shallots in olive oil for about 5 minutes over medium-high heat. Add thyme, rosemary, bay leaf, black pepper and cook for a few minutes longer. Add tomatoes and simmer over low heat for 20-40 minutes until tender and sweet. Adjust seasoning with kosher salt, sugar and a touch of cream to taste. Puree in blender or food processor.

Chef: Corey Mattson

Rice Paper Wrapped Tuna with Ginger Sauce

Serves 4

Tuna:

4	6-oz. tuna steaks (sushi grade)
8	rice paper eggroll wrappers (2 per steak)
1	beaten egg for all
	salt and red pepper mixed together

Ginger Sauce:

1/2 cup	white wine
pinch	red pepper flakes
1 oz.	honey
1 TB	lemon juice
1 1/2 TB	soy sauce
1 1/2 TB	olive oil
1 TB	ginger, chopped
1/8 tsp.	garlic, crushed
2 tsp.	arrowroot
1 oz.	apple juice

• **PROCEDURE**

Ginger sauce:

Boil together over medium-high heat, wine, red pepper, honey, lemon juice, soy, olive oil, ginger and garlic. After 1-2 minutes, add arrowroot and apple juice. Continue boiling for 1 minute. Set aside and reserve.

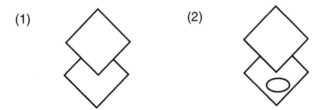

Tuna:

(1) Lay out rice paper as shown and brush with eggwash. Partially slice tuna steak in half without cutting all the way through and fold together. (2) Place folded tuna on bottom half of rice paper, (3) roll up one turn, (4) then fold side flaps over tuna (right and left). Repeat roll and fold technique until (5) rice paper has rolled into a cylinder. Set aside until ready to cook.

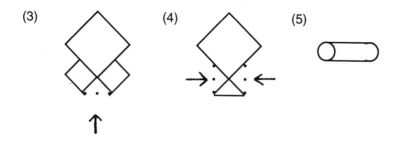

(3)   (4)   (5)

— Heat a pot of vegetable oil to 400 degrees. Fry each wrapped piece of tuna for 4 minutes. Remove and let rest for 2 minutes, then slice 4 times, creating 5 medallions from each. Serve with Ginger Dipping Sauce, stir-fried julienned vegetables and Japanese rice.

• **WINE SELECTION**

This dish deserves a good Alsatian Riesling, in particular Hugel 1989 Riesling Jubilee. The ginger in the dish is accented well by the delicateness of the riesling. The wine's age and great, ripe vintage give it a hint of apple and litchi berry on the nose, and these aromatic qualities bring out the flavor in the dish.

Chef: Corey Mattson

Rice Paper Wrapped Tuna with Ginger Sauce

Soft-shell Crayfish over Cheese Grits

This is a wonderful appetizer or entree, a truly Southern dish. Corey suggests making the grits first as they will hold their heat better. When making orange juice reduction, reduce to at least 1/5th of original volume. (A good tip is to do 1 quart a day ahead of time.) The sauce for the crayfish will break if it remains in a very hot pan, so if you can't pour it immediately, store in a warm gravy boat.

Serves 4

Crayfish:

4 tsp.	cajun spice mix
1/2 cup	flour
1/2 cup	cornmeal
1-2 TB	olive oil
1 TB	orange juice, reduced
1 TB	softened butter
1 tsp.	parsley, chopped
16-20	crayfish (4-6 per person)

Grits:

1 cup	water
2 oz.	grits
pinch	salt, cayenne, black pepper
2	scallions, minced
1/4 lb.	sharp cheddar cheese, grated

• PROCEDURE

Crayfish:

Toss crayfish in a mixture of flour and cornmeal. Saute in a fry pan coated with olive oil over medium heat for a few minutes until crayfish turn bright orange. Place on paper towel or colander to drain. Pour off any remaining oil from pan. Add the Cajun spice to pan and let cook for about 15 seconds. Add butter and orange juice reduction. Stir and bring to a simmer. Add chopped parsley.

Grits:

Combine water and grits in a saucepan over medium heat stirring constantly until thick and overcooked. Add salt, cayenne, black pepper, minced scallions and cheddar cheese. Stir until evenly mixed.

• To serve

Use an ice cream scoop to place a ball of grits in center of the plate. Arrange crayfish on top of grits, pour sauce over crayfish and serve.

Chef: Corey Mattson

Mixed Grill of Quail, Lamb, and Veal with Waffle-cut Potatoes and Balsamic Vinaigrette

Serves 4

1/2 lb.	mesculun mix (gourmet greens)
4	quail
4	veal medallions
4	lamb chops
6 cloves	shallots, finely chopped
1	small carrot, peeled and shredded
1	stalk celery, peeled and chopped
3 cups	red wine
1	bay leaf
pinch	fennel seed
3	freshly cracked white peppercorns
pinch	sage
	kosher salt to taste
5	large Idaho potatoes
	olive oil (to fry potatoes)
1/3 cups	balsamic vinegar
1 TB	honey
1	scallion, minced
1 TB	orange zest, minced
1 cup	olive oil
	fresh edible flowers or fruit segments for garnish

• Procedure

Preheat oven to 375 degrees.

— Rub quail with sage and salt, rub veal with fennel and salt, and lamb chops with white pepper and salt.

— Coat a shallow roasting pan with just enough olive oil to glaze the pan. Brown all pieces of meat on all sides and remove. Add chopped

178

vegetables, seasonings and bay leaf. Stir until pan is clean of browning residue. Add wine and simmer until wine is half gone. Add meat and place in oven for 5-10 minutes.

— Remove from oven. Reserve meat. Quail should be completely cooked, veal medium, lamb chops medium-rare. Strain pan drippings and reserve.

— Peel potatoes and cut in waffles or thin slices. Fry until golden brown and reserve on paper towels. Salt and pepper to taste.

Vinaigrette:
In blender combine balsamic vinegar, honey, scallion and orange zest. Trickle in oil while machine is running. (Note: this will make more vinaigrette than needed, but it is difficult to make it well if less ingredients are used.)

To serve:
Toss mesculun with about 1/3 cup vinaigrette split onto 4 large chilled plates. Arrange chips and meat on and around greens. Drizzle the roasting pan liquid over the meat and greens. Garnish with edible flowers or fresh fruit segments.

Chef: Corey Mattson

Sauteed Halibut over Roasted Fennel with Red Pepper and Kalamata Olive Tapenade

Serves 4

4	5-oz. halibut portions
2	fennel bulbs, julienned
1 TB	fresh rosemary, chopped
1/2 cup	olive oil
2	red peppers, peeled and diced small
1 cup	Kalamata olives, split lengthwise
1 TB	capers
1	garlic clove, crushed
1/2 cup	extra virgin olive oil
1/4 cup	white wine
1 tsp.	lemon juice
1 TB	parsley, chopped
	salt and pepper to taste

• **PROCEDURE**

Preheat oven to 375 degrees.

— Toss julienned fennel with 1/2 cup olive oil, season with rosemary, salt, and pepper. Cover with foil and roast in preheated oven for 25 minutes. Remove, strain and reserve fennel in a warm location.

— Saute garlic in olive oil over medium heat. Do not brown. Add diced red peppers and split olives and continue cooking for an additional minute. Add white wine and simmer for 3 minutes.

— Finish tapenade with lemon juice, salt, pepper and parsley.

— Season halibut with salt and pepper and saute until medium-rare. Remove from heat and hold in warm place.

• **TO SERVE**

Place a bed of warm fennel on each plate and top with a portion of halibut. Spoon tapenade over halibut and around fennel. Serve immediately.

• **WINE SELECTION**

The olives and peppers add a Mediterranean essence to this dish, making it a natural for a wine from the south of France, such as Bandol Rose from Domaine Tempier. This rose has a wonderful fruit and pronounced earthiness that gives spice to the olives and peppers and still enhances the fish.

Chef: Eric Lampe

Oven Roasted Plum Strudel with Port Wine Ice Cream

Serves 8

Plum filling:
12	black or red plums
1 cup	sugar

Strudel:
1 pkg.	phyllo dough
1 cup	butter
1/2 cup	sugar
2 cups	walnuts
1 tsp.	ground pepper
1/2 tsp.	salt

Caramel sauce:
3/4 cup	sugar
1/2 cup	light corn syrup
1 cup	heavy cream
3 TB	butter

Port wine ice cream:
1 bottle	port wine
2 cups	heavy cream
1 cup	milk
6	egg yolks
3/4 cup	sugar
1	vanilla bean, split lengthwise

Garnish:
1 pt.	blackberries
	mint sprigs

• PROCEDURE

Plum filling:

Preheat oven to 350 degrees.

— Wash and quarter plums. Arrange on a cooling rack and place on sheet pan. Sprinkle with sugar and bake at 350 degrees for approximately 20-30 minutes. (This will concentrate the plum flavor and help to drain off excess liquid.) Allow to cool.

Strudel:

Brown butter in a saute pan over moderate heat. Remove when the butter is foamy and has a nutty smell. In a food processor, grind the walnuts, sugar, salt and pepper until fine. Unroll the phyllo and brush 1 sheet with brown butter. Repeat with a second sheet, and sprinkle generously with the walnut mixture. Cover with another sheet of phyllo, brushing with more butter. Repeat 2 times, for a total of 5 sheets (2 plain, 3 with nuts). Spoon 1/2 of the plum filling along the long edge of the strudel, roll in a cylinder and brush the outside with butter. Sprinkle with walnut mixture. Repeat until all the plum filling is used. Bake the strudel at 350 degrees until golden brown, about 30-40 minutes.

Port wine ice cream:

In a heavy sauce pan, reduce the port wine with the vanilla bean until it reaches a syrupy consistency. Add the cream and milk and bring to a boil. Whisk the egg yolks and sugar together. Add 1/2 of the boiling cream mixture to the yolks, mixing thoroughly. Return the yolk mixture to the cream on the stove and cook over moderate heat until the custard coats the back of a spoon. Remove from heat, strain, and cool in an ice bath. Freeze in an ice cream maker according to manufacturer's directions.

Caramel sauce:

In a heavy sauce pan, combine the sugar and corn syrup. Clean the sides of the pan with a spatula so that no sugar remains. Cook over high heat until the sugar is a light brown (like iced tea). Remove from heat and add the cream VERY carefully (it will splatter). Return to heat, bring to boil, remove from stove, and stir in butter.

• To assemble

Slice the strudel diagonally. Pour the caramel sauce onto the plates, arrange strudel on sauce, and top with port wine ice cream. Garnish with fresh blackberries and mint if desired.

Chef: Heather Mendenhall

Frozen B-52 Parfait

This is a very elegant frozen parfait. The Florentine tuiles are thin crisp cookies that when made into different shapes make the dessert very attractive.

Frozen B-52 Parfait

Bailey's custard:

4	egg yolks
1/4 cup	sugar
1/4 cup	water
1/2 cup	Bailey's Irish Cream
1 cup	cream
2 tsp.	instant coffee, dissolved in 1 tsp. hot water

Grand Marnier custard:

4	egg yolks
1/4 cup	sugar
1/4 cup	water
1/2 cup	Grand Marnier
1 cup	cream

Florentine tuiles:

5 oz.	egg whites
5 oz.	powdered sugar
4 oz.	all purpose flour
3 oz.	melted butter
1/2 cup	toasted almonds, slivered
	zest of 3 oranges

Garnish:

	chocolate sauce
	orange segments

• PROCEDURE

Parfait:

Whip yolks in a mixer at high speed. Bring the sugar and water to a boil while whipping yolks. Add the boiling syrup to the whipping yolks in a steady stream. Allow to whip until light and foamy and mixer bowl is cool to the touch. Mix in Bailey's Cream and dissolved coffee. Scrape the yolk mixture into a large bowl, whip the cream to soft peaks and fold together until smooth. Repeat the procedure with the Grand Marnier recipe. Marble the two parfaits together and freeze in a 10-inch spring form pan or standard bread loaf. If you use a loaf pan, line it first with plastic wrap. Freeze for at least 6 hours or overnight.

Florentine tuiles:

Preheat oven to 350 degrees.

— In a food processor, grind together the almonds, orange zest and powdered sugar until fine. Whip the egg whites to stiff peaks, add the nut mixture to the whites and whip (the whites will fall). Add the flour and butter to the whites and whip until well incorporated. Spread the tuile batter thinly onto baking parchment in circles, approximately 6 inches in diameter. Bake until golden, about 10 minutes. Form into desired shapes while still hot—for example, for a bow tie shape, simply pinch the center together and twist slightly.

• **To** SERVE
Slice parfait with a knife dipped in hot water. Arrange on a plate with Florentine cookies, chocolate sauce, if desired, and orange segments.

Chef: Heather Mendenhall

411 West

Address: 411 West Franklin St.
Phone: 976-2782
Hours: Lunch: Monday-Friday 11:30 a.m.-2:30 p.m.
      Saturday 11:30 a.m.-4 p.m.
      Dinner: Monday-Thursday 5-10 p.m.
      Friday-Saturday 5-10:30 p.m.
      Sunday 5:30-10 p.m.
V,P,N,NC,2
Credit cards: Amex/Din/Dis/MC/Visa

When you arrive at 411, you are greeted with the fabulous aroma from the wood-fired pizza oven. Then your attention is drawn to the sophisticated decor with it's peach stucco walls, cloud-painted ceiling, arched picture window, skylight and exotic plants.

411 is called an Italian cafe and is well known for it's pizzettes bearing such ingredients as artichoke hearts, goat cheese, marinated chicken, Italian sausage, beef tenderloin, plum tomatoes, gorgonzola and much more. There also is wood-fired focaccia bread with a choice of artichoke dip, salsa fresca or sun-dried tomato.

Pastas are available in full or half orders at 411 and include Black Pepper Papardelle (wide ribbon pasta with freshly smoked salmon, dill cream sauce and parmesan) and Lasagna. Entrees include Chicken Marsala and Wood Grilled Beef Tenderloin with Herb Parmesan Crust and Chianti Glaze.

Chef Trey Cleveland, who was raised in New Orleans and trained at Culinary Institute of America, left 411 early in 1997, and as this book was going to press, no new chef had been named.

411 West Gazpacho

Gazpacho is a traditional Italian soup and can be served hot or cold.

Serves 8-12

1 cup	carrots, diced
1/4 cup	onion, diced
1/2 cup	zucchini, diced
1/4 cup	green pepper, diced
1 tsp.	fresh thyme
1 tsp.	fresh oregano
1 tsp.	fresh basil
1/4 cup	olive oil
1	large celery stalk, diced
1/2 cup	yellow squash, diced
1/2 cup	cucumber, diced
1/4 cup	red pepper, diced
1 tsp.	minced garlic
4 cups	water or vegetable stock
1 tsp.	Tabasco
1 TB	fresh lemon juice
3 cups	tomato juice

• PROCEDURE

Dice all vegetables about 1/4-inch square. Place vegetables along with the finely chopped herbs in a large bowl and set aside. Simmer olive oil and garlic in a large pan over low heat about 1 minute. Add water or stock, lemon juice and Tabasco and bring to a boil. When water is at a boil, pour over vegetables in the bowl and let stand for 5 minutes. Add tomato juice and mix thoroughly. Chill or serve warm.

Chef: Trey Cleveland

Crostini Marguerite

This is a lovely salad or appetizer and is often featured on the 411 menu.

Serves 4

4	toasted crostini (pumpernickel bread works well)
12 slices	smoked mozzarella
4 cups	marinated roma tomatoes (marinade recipe follows)
1 1/4 cups	baby greens
	parsley for garnish

Marinade:

4 TB	chopped basil
4 TB	balsamic vinegar
4 TB	olive oil
	salt and pepper to taste

• PROCEDURE

Toast the bread lightly, cut into triangles, and remove the crusts before serving. Place 3 slices of the mozzarella on the crostini and put into a 450-degree oven for 2 minutes to crisp the bread and melt the cheese. Dice the roma tomatoes in large pieces and marinate for at least 2 hours.

— To serve, arrange about 1/4 cup baby greens on a plate and place the crostini in the middle. Ladle the marinated tomatoes over the crostini and garnish with parsley.

Chef: Trey Cleveland

Pan Seared Tuna with Double Cream Gorgonzola Sauce and Fried Onions

This is a terrific entree. Sushi-grade tuna must be used since the fish is served seared and rare. Sushi-grade tuna can be found at the Fresh Market or at Well Spring. Call about availability.

Serves 4-6

4-6	6-oz. tuna steaks
1/2 cup	tomatoes, finely chopped, for garnish

Sauce:

1/2 cup	lobster broth (canned clam juice may be substituted)
1 tsp.	shallots, minced
1/2 cup	heavy cream
4 TB	butter
1/4 cup	white wine
1/4 cup	gorgonzola cheese

Fried onions:

4 cups	flour
2 tsp.	pepper
1 cup	water
2 qt.	canola oil
1 TB	salt
1	egg
4 cups	red onion, sliced

• PROCEDURE

Tuna:

The skillet must be very hot; use a high flame. Sprinkle the fish with salt, pepper and a touch of olive oil on both sides and sear until golden brown on both sides.

Sauce:

In a sauce pan, reduce the broth, wine and shallots by 1/2. Add cream and reduce again until thick. Whip in the butter and cheese to finish.

Onions:

Mix salt and pepper with the flour. Mix eggs and water. Dredge the onions in flour, then in egg wash, then in flour again. Fry onions in small batches until crispy and brown and drain on paper towel before serving.

• To SERVE
Place the tuna on the plate. Drizzle the sauce over the tuna and garnish with onions and tomatoes.

• WINE SELECTION
Port goes well with gorgonzola, but it's far too overwhelming for tuna. So what's the next best thing? Zinfandel! A very ripe red zinfandel from a great producer can be almost port-like, especially one from Ridge Pagani Ranch, the best zinfandel producer by far. The ripeness and concentration of this wine are like that of no other. They enhance the gorgonzola, yet don't overwhelm the delicateness of the tuna. In fact, the wine's cedary nose and intense spice complement the fish quite nicely.

Chef: Trey Cleveland

Chicken Cacciatori

Trey says this is an excellent recipe for busy cooks because it also can be made in a crock pot and left to cook.

Serves 4-6

2 lb.	chicken breasts
1 cup	onion, diced
1 TB	dry basil
2	bay leaves
4 cups	chicken stock, or unsalted canned chicken broth
1 cup	red wine
2 TB	olive oil
2 lb.	boneless chicken thighs
2 cups	sliced mushrooms
1 TB	dry oregano
1 tsp.	black pepper

• PROCEDURE

Preheat oven to 400 degrees.

— In a hot skillet with 1 tsp. of oil, brown off the chicken on both sides. Remove the chicken and in the same skillet saute the onions, mushrooms and herbs for 3 minutes. If you are cooking in the oven, bring the rest of the ingredients to a boil and add the chicken. Place in the oven and cook until chicken is very tender—about 1 1/2 hours. If you are using a crock pot, after browning the chicken, place all ingredients in the pot and cook on medium-high for 4-6 hours.

Chef: Trey Cleveland

Almond Cookies for Gelato and Sorbet

Trey was kind enough to share his grandmother's recipe for almond cookies. 411 serves them with sorbet. You may also serve with gelato or ice cream.

1 lb.	almond paste
1 lb.	sugar
6	egg whites

• PROCEDURE

Preheat oven to 325 degrees.

— In a large mixing bowl with a paddle, thoroughly mix together almond paste and sugar. Add the egg whites 1 at a time, until fully incorporated. Using 1-oz. scoops, drop onto paper-lined sheet pan and bake until golden brown. Let cool before serving. This dough can also be shaped into cylinders before cooking.

Chef: Trey Cleveland

Strawberry Amaretto Frozen Mousse Pie

This pie is very smooth and should be cut when frozen. It is best to use a 10-inch spring form pan.

Yields 1 pie

6	egg yolks
3 cups	heavy cream
3/4 cup	sugar
1 cup	strawberry preserves
2 TB	almond extract

Crust:

1 1/2 cups	graham cracker crumbs
1/3 cup	sugar
1/2 cup	melted butter

• PROCEDURE

Combine egg yolks and strawberry preserves in a large metal bowl and whisk together. Place the bowl over a pot of simmering water (double boiler) and whisk continuously until it becomes thick. Remove from heat and whisk until cool—about 5 minutes. In a large mixing bowl, beat the cream, almond extract and sugar until stiff peaks appear. Gently fold the cream mixture with a rubber spatula into the egg mixture, a small amount at a time.

Crust:

Preheat oven to 375 degrees.

— Mix all ingredients and press to the bottom of the spring form pan with your fingertips. If it will not adhere, add a touch more melted butter. Bake the crust for about 6 minutes.

— When crust is cool, pour the filling into the pan and freeze for 4 hours or overnight. You may garnish with fresh strawberries and/or whipped cream.

Chef: Trey Cleveland

IL PALIO RISTORANTE

Address: 1505 E. Franklin St.
Phone: 929-4000
Hours: Daily 6-10 p.m.
E,V,P,N,S,D,4
Credit cards: Amex/MC/Visa

Il Palio Ristorante, nestled in the elegant Sienna Hotel, holds the area's only Four Diamond Award.

The decor is reminiscent of a 15th century castle. Hand-carved arm chairs, beveled mirrors, and marble floors adorn the foyer. Baroque columns, tapestries, figurines, and chandeliers, decorate the dining room.

Because the restaurant is in the hotel, it serves breakfast, brunch, lunch and dinner. It is a beautiful spot for weddings, receptions and corporate functions.

The menu is northern Italian, using mostly Tuscan ingredients, infused oils and fresh herbs.

Chef Brian Stapelton, a California native, has 16 years of professional cooking experience in Atlanta, Palm Beach, Boston and St. Louis.

Pastas, risottos and gnocchis are offered as either appetizer or entree at Il Patio. As appetizer, you might try Cavatelle con Funghi (small shell pasta with wild mushrooms and asiago cheese with basil oil), Gnocchi con Capesante (potato dumplings with scallops, Pernod, and lobster butter) or Polenta con Sasiccia (white cornmeal, chicken, apple, sausage and rosemary). You might follow your appetizer with Minestra con fagioli (Tuscan white bean soup with smoked ham) or Insalata al la Cessare (Caesar salad tossed tableside). For entrees you can choose from items such as Filetto di Franzino con Risotto (fillet of Black Grouper over golden potato risotto with basil and red pepper oil) or Cosciotto di Angello (lamb shank with creamy herb polenta and beet infused lamb jus).

— recipes shared —

Sweet Potato Gnocci, Creamy Nutmeg and Spinach
Osso Bucco
Seared Black Grouper and Golden Potato Risotto
with Red and Yellow Pepper Oil
Orange Mango Gelato

Sweet Potato Gnocchi, Creamy Nutmeg and Spinach

Serves 4

2 lb.	sweet potatoes
2 1/2 cups	all-purpose flour
1	egg
	salt and pepper to taste
1/4 cup	sugar
1 tsp.	nutmeg
1 cup	cream
1 clove	garlic
1	medium shallot, finely diced
1 cup	chicken stock
1/2 bunch	spinach

Sweet Potato Gnocchi, Creamy Nutmeg and Spinach

• PROCEDURE

Peel sweet potatoes. Combine flour, egg, 1/2 sugar, 1/2 nutmeg, salt and pepper. Place sweet potatoes in boiling water and cook until soft. Remove and let steam for 5 minutes. While potatoes are still warm, puree them in a food processor. Add flour mix and combine thoroughly, being careful not to overmix. Roll the resulting dough into a long strip. Portion into 1/2-inch pieces and roll on fork to create ridges. Set aside gnocchi.

Sauce:

In saute pan, saute finely diced shallot and garlic. Add chicken stock and reduce by half. Add heavy cream and reduce by half again. Season sauce with remaining sugar, nutmeg, salt and pepper.
— Place gnocchi in boiling water and cook until done. Add to sauce. Garnish with fresh spinach.

Chef: Brian Stapleton

Osso Bucco

Serves 4-6

4	veal shanks
8 oz.	risotto
2 pinches	saffron
3	medium carrots, peeled, chopped
3 stalks	celery, chopped
1	medium shallot, minced
1 clove	garlic, minced
4 cups	chicken stock
1/2 cup	reggiano cheese
1 TB	butter
1/4 cup	olive oil
2 qt.	veal stock (reduced canned beef broth may be substituted)
1	lemon
1 cup	sugar
4 sprigs	thyme
4 sprigs	rosemary
	salt
	peppercorn
2	bay leaves

• **PROCEDURE**

Finely chop herbs, combine lemon juice and sugar to marinate veal overnight.

— Preheat oven to 300 degrees.

— Cook celery, carrots and shallots with olive oil in a hot, thick-bottomed saute pan for 4-5 minutes.

— Season veal shanks with salt and cracked black pepper. Add to pan. Continue to cook until shanks are brown on both sides. Add red wine and cook until reduced by 3/4ths.

— Add veal stock until shanks are completely covered. Cover and cook in 300-degree oven for 2-3 hours.

— Remove from oven and leave shanks in cooking liquid.

Saffron risotto:

Combine saffron with chicken stock and bring to a boil. Once stock is flavored, strain and keep warm. Over high heat, saute shallots, garlic and risotto until rice is slightly roasted.

— Add 1/2 saffron stock to the risotto and bring to a boil. Stir and add

remainder of stock as needed until rice is done (about 20 minutes).
— Add reggiano cheese, butter, salt and pepper. Serve immediately.

• WINE SELECTION
A merlot-based Saint Emilion from France would complement this classic entree. Along with the merlot grape you will also find some cabernet and cabernet franc—which meld wonderfully with the ingredients in this dish—in a wine such as the Chateau, La Couronne 1993.

Chef: Brian Stapleton

Osso Bucco

Seared Black Grouper and Golden Potato Risotto with Red and Yellow Pepper Oil

Serves 4

28 oz.	grouper
1/2	red bell pepper
1/2	yellow bell pepper
2 cloves	garlic
4	medium golden potatoes
1 bunch	spinach
2 cups	chicken stock
2	medium shallots
1 TB	butter
2 oz.	reggiano cheese
1 cup	olive oil

• **PROCEDURE**

Clean and rinse spinach. Set aside. Peel and finely dice golden potatoes. Store in water.

— Coarsely chop red pepper. Blend thoroughly with 4 oz. of olive oil, small amount of garlic, salt and pepper. Repeat process with yellow pepper, keeping the pepper oils separate.

— Portion grouper into 2.5-oz. medallions (3 medallions per person). Set aside.

Potato risotto:

Saute shallots, garlic and diced potatoes in olive oil in hot pan. Continue to saute for 3 minutes. Add 1/2 the chicken stock and bring to a boil. Continue to add stock and cook until potatoes are done. Finish with reggiano cheese.

— Season grouper medallions with salt and pepper and sear on both sides until done. Braise spinach.

— To serve, place risotto on plate, then alternate layers of fish and spinach on top of risotto. Drizzle red and yellow pepper oil around grouper.

Grouper is always wonderful with wine. Its rich, meaty texture and delicate flavor are especially enhanced by white burgundy. A good choice
would be a straight Puligny-Montrachet from Etienne Sauzet. Any vintage will do. Sauzet is a consistent producer. This wine adds a nice
buttery character to the fish as well as a light nutty flavor.

Chef: Brian Stapleton

Orange Mango Gelato

Serves 8

3	ripe to overripe mangos
1 1/2 cups	concentrated orange juice
1/3 cup	water
1/4 cup	triple sec
1/3 cup	sugar

• PROCEDURE

Peel mangos, remove pit. Puree in blender or food processor until they
have attained a smooth consistency.
— Add remaining ingredients, puree for approximately 3 minutes.
— Place in plastic container, freeze for at least 14 hours, making sure
container is tightly covered.

Chef: Brian Stapleton

LA RESIDENCE

Address: 202 W. Rosemary St.
Phone: 967-2506
Hours: Tuesday-Saturday 6-9:30 p.m.
        Sunday 6-9 p.m.
Credit cards: Amex/Din/MC/Visa

La Residence, otherwise known as La Rez, has been serving triangle diners for more than 20 years. Its first location was in what is now known as the Fearrington House. It now occupies a renovated 1920's house on Rosemary Street, just a few blocks from the campus of UNC. Each room of the nostalgic and attractive old house offers its own style, and, of course, there is the romantic courtyard for special events.

Head Chef Jackie Derey has worked at La Rez for nearly a decade. She is an avid gardener as well as a talented chef, and during the growing months she supplies the restaurant with a plethora of her own produce—herbs, tomatoes, eggplants, squashes, berries and edible flowers.

Originally from Charlotte, Jackie was the youngest of six daughters. As long as she can remember, she has been cooking. She spent time in Europe and the Midwest gaining experience before coming to La Rez.

The menus over which she presides vary seasonally and include such choices as Puree of White and Black Bean Soup, Softshell crabs with Caper Garlic Sauce, Whole Maine Lobster Salad with Lemon-lime Mayonnaise, and Crispy Duck and Vegetable Strudel with a Port Wine Roquefort Sauce. A wide range of dishes is always offered.

Carrot-orange Soup with Ginger

Serves 4-6

3 TB	butter or margarine
1	large onion, coarsely chopped
5	large fresh carrots, peeled and coarsely chopped
1 1/2 TB	flour
2 1/4 cups	chicken stock, or broth
1 cup	orange juice
1 tsp.	light brown sugar, packed
1	3-in. cinnamon stick
3/4 tsp.	fresh ginger, peeled and minced
1/8 tsp.	ground white pepper
3/4 cup	light cream, or half and half
	salt to taste
	fresh chives for garnish, finely chopped

• PROCEDURE

Melt the butter in a large saucepan over medium-high heat. Add the onion and carrots and cook, stirring constantly for 4-5 minutes or until onion is limp. Using a wooden spoon, stir in the flour until thoroughly incorporated and smooth. Continue stirring for a few minutes. Stir in the stock until well blended and smooth. Add the orange juice, brown sugar, cinnamon stick, ginger root, and pepper. Bring the mixture to a boil. Then lower the heat and simmer covered for about 15 minutes, or until carrots are tender. Discard the cinnamon stick. Set the pot aside to cool slightly.

— Transfer the mixture in batches to a blender. Blend on low speed for 10 seconds. Raise the speed to high and blend until completely pureed. Rinse out the pan previously used and pour the puree into it. Add the cream and salt. Heat the soup over medium-high heat, stirring occasionally, until piping hot but not boiling. Garnish each serving with a pinch of fresh chives.

Chef: Jackie Derey

203

Carrot Orange Soup with Ginger paired
with Provencale Stuffed Pork Loin

Provencale Stuffed Pork Loin

This is an attractive dish when colorful vegetables are used. Some good choices would be leeks, red and yellow peppers, carrots, zucchini, yellow squash and asparagus.

2-lb.	boneless pork loin, trimmed
	salt and pepper to taste
2 TB	fresh rosemary, chopped
3 TB	fresh thyme, chopped
1 TB	olive oil

Provencale:

5 cups	vegetables of your choice, chopped or julienned
1 TB	shallots, minced
1/2 tsp.	salt
2 tsp.	garlic, minced
1/2 tsp.	white pepper
1 TB	parsley, chopped
1/4 cup	olive oil

• PROCEDURE

Butterfly cut pork lion. Rub with olive oil, salt, pepper, and herbs. Cover with plastic wrap and let sit for 2-3 hours.

— Mix the vegetables with 3 TB of oil and let sit 30-40 minutes at room temperature. Add 1 TB oil to a hot skillet, cook vegetables 2-3 minutes, stirring constantly so they don't burn. Spread the vegetables on a baking sheet and finish in a 400-degree oven for 5-8 minutes. Let cool. Roll in plastic wrap to form a cylinder about 1-1/2 inches in diameter and freeze.

— Place the vegetable roll in the middle of the seasoned loin and wrap the pork loin snugly around it. Tie with butcher's twine to hold it together. Sear all sides in a hot pan with a small amount of oil.

— Place on a rack in a roasting pan. Roast at 375 degrees for 20-30 minutes, or until the internal temperature reaches 145 degrees. Remove from oven and let sit for 15 minutes before serving. Cut into pinwheels.

Chef: Jackie Derey

Hazelnut-Frangelico Pound Cake

Yields 1 Cake

12 oz.	butter
2 cups	sugar
1/2 tsp.	salt
6	large eggs
2 TB	Frangelico
1/3 cup	buttermilk
3 cups	cake flour
1 tsp.	baking powder
1 cup	hazelnuts, toasted and chopped

Glaze:

1/2 cup	water
1/2 cup	sugar
3 TB	Frangelico

• PROCEDURE

Preheat oven to 350 degrees.

— Cream together butter, sugar, and salt until smooth and slowly add one egg at a time on low speed. Then add Frangelico and buttermilk. Mix together the flour and baking powder and slowly add this to the wet mixture. Mix in the hazelnuts.

— Bake for one hour until a cake tester comes out clean.

Glaze:

Boil all ingredients, cool a bit, and pour over the cake.

Chef: Jackie Derey

Hazelnut-Frangelico Pound Cake

WEATHERVANE

Address: East Gate Shopping Center
Phone: 929-9466
Hours: Monday-Thursday 11 a.m.-10 p.m.
        Friday-Saturday 11 a.m.-11 p.m.
V,O,N,S,NC,2
Credit cards: Amex/MC/Visa

At Weathervane, Chef Devon Mills manages a successful restaurant that not only produces lunch and dinner but supplies the deli and bakery sections of A Southern Season nearby and the catering demands of both establishments.

Devon has worked in restaurants in the Triangle for more than 11 years, starting at La Residence when he was just out of high school. He worked alongside the owners' niece, who was down from Michigan for college. They are now married. After La Residence, Devon worked for Ben Barker at Magnolia, assisted in opening 411 West in Chapel Hill and returned to La Residence as executive chef before taking the helm at Weathervane.

Devon was raised by a mother who was a dietician and he incorporates the lessons he learned from her into his menus. He enjoys fresh seafood and vegetables and cooks with all of his senses. His food subsequently is very colorful and attractive as well as delicious.

The menu changes seasonally with some of the more popular items remaining. Specials featured on one summer day included Chilled Cantaloupe and Champagne Soup, Carrboro Farmers Market Tomato Sampler with Mozzarella and Balsamic Vinegar and Grilled Pork Tenderloin with Black Beans and Mango Chutney. The menu often includes appetizers such as Three Cheese Fritters, Grilled Eggplant Caponata, and entrees such as Grilled Ribeye with Ancho Chili, Black Bean and

Corn Salsa, Grilled Black Pepper Tuna, and Vegetable Pasta. Sandwiches such as Portabella Mushrooms with Grated Asiago, Baby Spinach and Roasted Red Pepper Aioli are also available.

Many restaurants in the Triangle have outside dining facilities but the Weathervane wins the award for the most attractive. It has fountains, an outdoor bar, and big umbrellas with dainty white lights for evening dining.

— recipes shared —
Foccacia with Chevre and Sun-dried Tomatoes
Mussels with Roasted Vegetable Relish and White Wine
Southern Shrimp Chowder
Grilled Asparagus and Corn Salad
with Roasted Pepper Vinaigrette
Triggerfish with Orzo and Garden Gazpacho

Foccacia with Chevre and Sun-dried Tomatoes

Foccacia is a wonderful Italian bread often served as an appetizer. Again, with this dish, you can be creative if you want and vary the toppings—roasted garlic spread, parmesan cheese or any other favorite ingredients. Some people prefer to dip this bread in marinara or other sauces.

Yields 1 14-inch foccacia

Dough:

14 oz.	warm water
2 tsp.	dry yeast
1/4 cup	wheat flour
4 cups	bread flour
1/4 cup	olive oil
1/2 TB	minced garlic
2 tsp.	kosher salt

Toppings:

1/4 cup	olive oil
1 1/2 TB	salt
1/4 cup	sun-dried tomatoes, slivered
4 oz.	chevre goat cheese

Foccacia

• Procedure

Proof yeast and warm water in bowl. Let sit for 8-10 minutes until yeast becomes activated. In electric mixer equipped with a mixing paddle, add yeast mixture. Slowly add bread flour and wheat flour until combined.

— Add olive oil, minced garlic and salt. Switch to dough hook and knead for approximately 5 minutes on low speed. Knead for another 5 minutes by hand. Place dough in a bowl lightly coated with olive oil. Cover with plastic wrap until doubled in volume, approximately 4 hours. (You can refrigerate dough overnight wrapped in plastic, if desired. Bring dough back to room temperature before proceeding to the next step.)

— Once the dough has doubled, knead it into a ball shape. Using a rolling pin, roll the dough into a circular shape until it is about 2/3-inch thick. Place on a baking sheet or sheet pan. Cover loosely with slightly moist towel and let rise 1 hour.

— Before baking, indent dough with tips of your fingers approximately 2/3-inch. Do this all over. These pockets will be used to trap olive oil and seasonings later. It will also keep the bread from rising excessively during baking.

— Rub dough with olive oil and sprinkle with salt. Indent sun-dried tomato slivers deeply into the dough. Bake at 400 degrees for 18 minutes, or until golden brown. Spread goat cheese over bread as it cools, but while it is still warm. Slice and serve immediately.

Chef: Devon Mills

Mussels with Roasted Vegetable Relish and White Wine

Serves 4 as appetizer, 2 as entree

50-60	mussels, cleaned and beard removed
1 head	fennel
1	eggplant
1	medium zucchini
1	medium yellow squash
1	small red onion
1/2 cup	olive oil
1/2 TB	salt
pinch	pepper
2 cups	white wine
1	lemon, juiced
1 TB	garlic, minced
2 TB	shallots, minced
1	large ripe tomato
3 TB	slivered Kalamata olives
	zest of one lemon

Mussels with Roasted Vegetable Relish

Preheat oven 350 degrees.

— Clean and prepare mussels. Core the fennel. Dice fennel, eggplant, zucchini, squash and onion in about 1/3-inch cubes. In a large bowl, toss the vegetables, olive oil, salt and pepper. Roast for 12 minutes or until vegetables begin to turn deep golden brown. Set aside. Zest the lemon and reserve for garnish.

— In a large saucepan bring wine, garlic and shallots to a rapid boil. Add mussels and cover until mussels open, about 2 to 3 minutes. Once the mussels have opened add roasted vegetables, juice of one lemon, and chopped fresh herbs. Stir well and divide among plates or bowls. Spoon over excess sauce. Garnish with tomatoes, olives and lemon zest.

Chef: Devon Mills

Southern Shrimp Chowder

Serves 6

1 TB	butter
1 cup	cream
1	yellow onion, diced
1 cup	shucked corn (about 2 ears)
2 stalks	celery, diced
1 1/2 cups	lima or butter beans
1	large carrot, peeled and diced
1 1/2 lb.	fresh shrimp, peeled (reserve shells for shrimp stock)
1	red pepper, diced
3	shallots, minced
1 TB	kosher salt
5	new potatoes, diced 1/2-in.
1 tsp.	ground white pepper
small pinch	cayenne
2 TB each	fresh chopped basil and tarragon
1 cup	white wine
2 TB.	lemon juice
4 1/2 cups	shrimp stock

• Procedure

Peel shrimp, chill and set aside (reserve shells for shrimp stock). In a

3-qt. sauce pot, melt butter and gently saute onions, celery, carrots, and red pepper over medium-low heat for approximately 4 minutes, or until vegetables are tender. Add shallots, new potatoes, cayenne and bay leaves. Add wine, bring to a simmer, and reduce wine by 1/3.

— Add shrimp stock and simmer over medium heat for 15-18 minutes, or until potatoes are tender. Add cream and simmer an additional three minutes. Add corn and lima beans and cook for 2 minutes or until lima beans are soft. Add shrimp, remaining seasonings and serve. Garnish with fresh chopped tomatoes.

Chef: Devon Mills

Grilled Asparagus and Corn Salad with Roasted Pepper Vinaigrette

Serves 4

1 lb.	asparagus, pencil-sized with ends snapped
4 ears	corn
1	large yellow onion
2 TB	honey
2 TB	olive oil
2 cup	assorted lettuces
	olive oil and lemon juice (for greens)

Vinaigrette:

1	very large red pepper, roasted
1	whole shallot
2 TB	lemon juice
1/3 cup	olive oil
pinch	salt and pepper
1/4 cup	chopped fresh basil

• **PROCEDURE**

Preheat grill.

— To roast the red pepper for the vinaigrette, simply rub with olive oil and place in a 400-degree oven for 15-20 minutes, turning occasionally until skin is welted all over. Cool, peel and set aside.

— In a large pot of boiling water, blanch asparagus for 1-2 minutes until tender. Do not overcook. Place the asparagus directly in ice water to stop the cooking process. Drain. Divide asparagus into 4 equal portions and align tip-to-tip. Place two small skewers sideways through asparagus for grilling.

— Husk four ears of corn and remove silk. Rub corn with olive oil and set aside. Slice onion into 3/4-inch round slices, keeping slices intact. Mix together honey and olive oil and coat onion slices. Set aside.

— Grill onions and corn until tender and they have obtained char marks. Grill asparagus for approximately 2 minutes per side. Remove corn from cob and roughly chop onions. For the vinaigrette, simply puree all of the ingredients together in a blender.

— To serve, pour the vinaigrette equally on four plates. Arrange asparagus. Toss onions and corn with the lettuce, olive oil, and lemon juice and place over the asparagus. Serve immediately.

Chef: Devon Mills

Triggerfish with Orzo and Garden Gazpacho

Serves 4

Gazpacho:

3	large very ripe tomatoes
1/4 cup	dry sherry
1/4 cup	cold water
	zest and juice of 1 lemon
1/4 cup	extra virgin olive oil
3 cloves	garlic, finely minced
1	small red onion, finely diced
1	cucumber
1	yellow pepper
1	green pepper
1	small zucchini
1	small yellow squash
1 TB	salt
1/2 tsp.	ground pepper
1/4 cup	chopped fresh oregano, marjoram or basil
	olive oil

Pasta:

2 cups	orzo pasta
	salted boiling water
1/4 cup	olive oil
	salt and pepper
1/2 cup	herbs (thyme, oregano, basil, marjoram), chopped

juice and zest of one lemon

Fish:

    4 6-oz. triggerfish fillets
       salt and white pepper

• PROCEDURE

Gazpacho:

Remove the seeds and finely chop the tomatoes and cucumber.
— Finely dice the red onion, green and yellow peppers, zucchini, and yellow squash. Combine all of the gazpacho ingredients, mixing them well, and let sit for at least 20 minutes in the refrigerator before serving.

Pasta:

Bring the salted water to a boil, cook pasta until tender and drain. Warm olive oil over low heat. In a bowl toss pasta with olive oil, fresh herbs, lemon juice and zest and salt and pepper to taste.

Fish:

Saute triggerfish in olive oil over medium-high heat for 2-3 minutes per side, lightly sprinkling with salt and white pepper. To serve, divide gazpacho sauce evenly on four plates, mound warm orzo in the center and place trigger fish on top of the orzo.

• WINE SELECTION

This dish leaves the door open to an abundance of wines, but the ultimate choice is the 1992 Oregon Pinot Noir Reserve from Elk Cove Vineyards. This is one of the most full-bodied pinots from Oregon with rich fruit, tannins, and great structure that is perfect with triggerfish, and the wine's light spice goes very well with the gazpacho.

Chef: Devon Mills

Other Chapel Hill
Restaurants of Note

Squid's
Address: 15-501 By-pass at Elliot Road
Phone: 942-8757
Hours: Monday-Thursday 5-9:30 p.m.
    Friday-Saturday 5-10 p.m.
    Sunday 5-9 p.m.
N,3
Credid cards: Amex/Din/Dis/MC/Visa

STOCKS AND SAUCES

STOCKS

Stocks are an intricate part of gourmet cooking. They are not difficult, but time is always needed for the reduction to remove excess liquid and produce flavor. Bones for making stocks are sometimes hard to find, but meat market managers will often provide them if asked. Get in the habit of freezing chicken, veal, beef and fish bones for later use in stocks.

Shrimp stock:

Yields about 1 qt.

8 cups	water
1 TB	butter
2-4 cups	shrimp shells and heads
2 TB	fresh diced tomatoes or tomato paste
1	onion, cut in 1/4ths
1	carrot, cleaned and coarsely cut
2	garlic cloves
1/2 cup	white wine

Saute the shells in the butter for a few minutes and add tomatoes. This brings out the rich flavor and color. Add all of the ingredients to the water. Bring to a boil for about 10-15 minutes, skimming off any impurities. Remove all the solids and reduce to about 4 cups.

Fish stock:

Yields about 1 1/2 qt.

10 lb.	fish bones (sea bass, red snapper, or similar types)
4 TB	butter, unsalted
2 stalks	celery, chopped
1	onion, peeled
1 bulb	fennel, peeled and chopped
1	leek, peeled and chopped
6 cloves	garlic, peeled and halved
2 cups	white wine

As with almost any stock, you may use any vegetables you may have to add flavor to your stock, such as green beans, carrots, etc. Saute the fish bones in butter for 5 minutes. Place in a large pot with the

217

vegetables and the wine. Boil 30 minutes, skimming away any impurities that rise to the top. Strain through cheesecloth and reduce to about 1 1/2 qt. May be frozen for later use.

Chicken stock:
Yields about 1 1/2 qt.

15 lb.	chicken bones
2	onions, peeled and chopped
2	carrots, peeled and chopped
4 stalks	celery, peeled and chopped
1 head	garlic, cut in half

As always, you may use additional vegetables of your choice. Place the chicken bones and vegetables in a large pot. Cover with cold water (about 5 qt.) and bring to a boil. Lower the heat and simmer for 4 hours, skimming away any impurities that rise to the top. Strain and reduce to about 1 1/2 quarts.

Veal stock:
Yields about 1 1/2 qt.

Use chicken stock recipe and replace chicken bones with veal bones.

Demi-glaze:
This is merely a reduction of the veal stock. Simply reduce for many hours until the sauce is a thicker consistency. Be careful not to scorch.

Sauces

Hollandaise:
Yields 2-3 cups

4-5	egg yolks
1 pt.	drawn butter
1-2 TB	fresh lemon juice
	dash or two of Tabasco to taste
	salt and white pepper to taste

You need to clarify the butter first by melting it and allowing the sediment to fall to the bottom. Remove the drawn butter from the top, discarding the sediment. It is best to remove the cords from the yolks in order to make for a smoother sauce. Cook in a double boiler over hot, not boiling water. First place the eggs over the heat and whisk continuously until the eggs are about 3 times their original size. Slowly ladle the drawn butter into the eggs, whisking to incorporate, until you have used all the butter. Slowly add the remaining ingredients to taste.

Bearnaise:

You will need all of the hollandaise ingredients, plus

1/2 cup	white wine
4 TB	red wine vinegar
2 TB	shallots, finely chopped
4 sprigs	tarragon, finely chopped
1 sprig	chervil, finely chopped
	additional lemon juice to taste

Simmer the above items over medium-high heat until reduced by 1/2. Remove and set aside. Follow the hollandaise recipe above and add the bearnaise ingredients slowly during the final steps.

Veloute:

Veloute is a white sauce made from a roux and stock base and used for soups and sauces.
Yields 1 1/2 cups

2 TB	butter
2 TB	flour
2 cups	stock (chicken, veal, fish or shellfish stock)
	(cream may substituted for a cream veloute)

In a double boiler (make sure not to use aluminum), melt the butter and slowly stir in the flour. After well blended, gradually add the stock. Stir until well combined and thickened, simmering slowly for about 1 hour.

RECIPE INDEX

221

Panned Breast of Free Range Chicken with Roasted Fingerling
Potatoes and Mushroom Chips with Port Caramel 105
Green Tabasco Baked Chicken 167
Chicken Cacciatori 190

Seafood:

Plantain Crusted Alaskan Halibut with Tarragon Butter 23
Lightly Dusted Lemon Peppered Salmon with Champagne Dill
Beurre Blanc finished with Smoked Salmon and Caviar.... 22
Pan Seared Tuna with Curried Citrus Vinaigrette and
Spicy Cous-cous Salad 29
Grouper in Potato Horseradish Crust 41
Roasted Swordfish Loin with Curried Potato Puree,
Asparagus Tips and Parsley Sauce 54
Vogie's Cajun Ettouffee 67
Asian Mustard Crusted Wild Striped Bass with Ginger Slaw 76
Potato Crusted Salmon with Tarragon Cream Sauce 78
Saffron Rubbed Grilled Jumbo Scallops with White Corn
and Haricot Vertes Risotto 86
Seared Tiger Shrimp with Roasted Tomato and
Artichoke Sauce over Romano Crusted Bread 89
Poached Red Snapper with Julienned Vegetables and
Honey-sage Sauce 102
Grilled Triggerfish with Tomato Basil Essence 109
Pickled Shrimp with Crab and Pepper Slaw and
Smoked Tomato Remoulade 136
Red Chili Scallops with Spicy Ginger Shrimp Sauce 123
Halibut with Crab and Pancetta Hash and Grapefruit Vinaigrette . 161
Rice Paper Wrapped Tuna with Ginger Sauce 175
Sauteed Halibut over Roasted Fennel with Red Pepper
and Kalamata Olive Tapenade.. 180
Pan Seared Tuna with Double Cream Gorgonzola Sauce
and Fried Onions 189
Seared Black Grouper and Golden Potato Risotto with
Red and Yellow Pepper Oil... 199
Triggerfish with Orzo and Garden Gazpacho 214

Pasta:

Parisian Shellfish Pan Roast over Angel Hair Pasta with
Roasted Garlic, Tomato, and Saffron Sauce...................... 80
Linguini with Green-lip Mussels and Littleneck Clams................. 129

Vegetarian:

Rigatoni a la Vodka 48
White Lasagna 74

BREADS

DESSERTS

MISCELLANEOUS